GOD, GENDER AND THE BIBLE

How can contemporary studies of gender and power illuminate the conflict between divine omnipotence and human
autonomy?

Deborah Sawyer discusses this crucial yet unresolved question in the
context of contemporary and postmodern ideas about gender and
power, based on fresh examination of a number of texts from Hebrew
and Christian scripture.

Such texts offer striking parallels to contemporary gender theories (particularly those of Luce Irigaray and Judith Butler), which
have unravelled given notions of power and constructed identity.
Through the study of gender in terms of its application by biblical
writers as a theological strategy, we can observe how these writers
use female characters to undermine human masculinity, through
their 'higher' intention to elevate the biblical God.

God, Gender and the Bible demonstrates that both maleness and
femaleness are constructed in the light of divine omnipotence.
Unlike many approaches to the Bible that offer hegemonist interpretations, such as those that are explicitly Christian or Jewish, or
liberationist or feminist, this enlightening and readable study
sustains and works with the inconsistencies evident in biblical literature.

Deborah F. Sawyer is Senior Lecturer in Biblical Studies in the
Department of Religious Studies at Lancaster University. Her recent
publications include *Women and Religion in the First Christian
Centuries* (Routledge 1996) and (co-edited) *Is There A Future For
Feminist Theology?* (1999).

D0162340

BIBLICAL LIMITS
Series editors:
David Gunn, *Texas Christian University, USA*
Gary A. Phillips, *Sewanee, The University of the South, USA*

KNOCKIN' ON HEAVEN'S DOOR
The Bible and popular culture
Roland Boer

THE BOOK OF HIDING
Gender, ethnicity, annihilation and Esther
Timothy K. Beal

READING BIBLES, WRITING BODIES
Identity and the book
edited by Timothy K. Beal and David Gunn

JESUS FRAMED
George Aichele

RACIALIZING JESUS
Race, ideology and the formation of modern
biblical scholarship
Shawn Kelley

GOD, GENDER AND THE BIBLE

Deborah F. Sawyer

London and New York

FOR SARA AND JENNIFER
IN SISTERHOOD THROUGH NATURE
AND NURTURE

First published 2002
by Routledge
11 New Fetter Lane, London EC4P 4EE

Simultaneously published in the USA and Canada
by Routledge
29 West 35th Street, New York, NY 10001

Routledge is an imprint of the Taylor & Francis Group

© 2002 Deborah F. Sawyer

Typeset in Garamond by
Florence Production Ltd, Stoodleigh, Devon
Printed and bound in Great Britain by
TJ International Ltd, Padstow, Cornwall

British Library Cataloguing in Publication Data
A catalogue record for this book is available from the British Library

Library of Congress Cataloging in Publication Data
A catalog record for this book has been requested

ISBN 0–415–17483-X (hbk)
ISBN 0–415–17484–8 (pbk)

CONTENTS

CONTENTS

ACKNOWLEDGEMENTS

The material that makes up this book has developed over a number of years, and follows on from many of the issues raised in *Women and Religion in the First Christian Centuries* (1996). Many of the ideas have been tested in various sections of the American Academy of Religion's and Society of Biblical Literature's joint Annual Meetings (1997–2000) – in particular, the AAR's 'History of Christianity' section and the SBL's 'Women in the Biblical World', 'Reading, Theory and the Bible' and 'Pauline Epistles'. My thanks go to the many individuals at those meetings who listened and who offered helpful suggestions. Earlier versions of my work on Jeremiah appeared in the *Journal for the Study of the Old Testament*, on Judith in *Feminist Theology* and *Theology and Sexuality*, and on Abraham in the *Expository Times*. Full references are given in the bibliography. My husband, John Sawyer, as ever, offered his unfailing support throughout the enterprise in ensuring I had time to work through these ideas, and in providing his invaluable advice. My son Joseph also deserves a big 'thank you' for not always complaining when his mother was preoccupied with a computer or a book rather than him.

In this volume all English extracts from the Bible are taken from the New Revised Standard Version (London: HarperCollins). Where an emphasis occurs in these extracts it is my own and is intended to highlight the particular word or phrase that has been selected by the biblical writer.

1

PRELIMINARY OBSERVATIONS

In her collection of essays on sex and citizenship, *The Queen of America Goes to Washington City*, Lauren Berlant asks this question, 'Are naïve infantile citizenship and paralysed cynical apathy the only positions a normal or moral American can assume?' (1997: 29). On reading Berlant's book I was struck by how those two positions could be descriptive of contemporary attitudes to the Bible. Despite being the most prescriptive single text in the formation of western and colonial politics and culture, nowadays it is ignored by the majority who allow it no conscious impact on their lives. But for the minority for whom it remains their constant guide through life, it attracts total commitment in defiance of its primitive world-view and archaic laws. Furthermore, Berlant's term, 'infantile citizenship', resonates with the consistent imperative evident across the many and varied texts of Bible itself, and that is the call for childlike obedience in recognition of the omnipotence of the parent. In contrast to Berlant's study, in my analysis of citizenship within the theocracies of biblical imagination, God replaces George Washington as the benevolent patriarch and the boundaries of the nation are cosmic.

The motivation for this volume is of course a selfish one. Over many years of studying and teaching biblical texts my ambivalence towards them has grown rather than diminished, centring on the tension between a ruthless discourse on divine power and an alternative discourse that suggests a positive notion of human autonomy. This ambivalence has been creative in foregrounding for me the issue, or problem, of omnipotence, and in doing so, paradoxically, has suggested alternative models for resistance and power. The central thesis of this study is twofold: to expose and explore the uncompromising and radical nature of the biblical call to faith; and to uncover the inconsistencies that posit alternative stances that can be explicit, but are consistently inferred as counter-possibilities

1

to the absolutism of omnipotence. Thus, although biblical texts will be subject to deconstruction and understood in the light of their own socio-political context, texts that infer a counter-culture, in relation to both the boundaries of their time and those of the Bible itself, will be brought to the fore. Such texts offer striking parallels to contemporary theoretical thought that effectively unravel given notions of power and constructed identity. This study attempts to work with the inconsistencies evident in biblical literature, and to maintain a critical awareness of the consistent assertion of divine omnipotence that is the hallmark of all texts.

'The Bible' is a mercurial title that can mean the Jewish scriptures, the Septuagint, the Christian Bible, the Protestant Bible or the Catholic Bible. Each book is different, and each in its entirety represents a particular set of beliefs or world-view. In this study numerous biblical texts are referred to and a number are examined in detail, and, where it is relevant, a particular text's place in a specific canon of scripture is discussed. The texts selected for this study are taken from the Hebrew Bible, the Jewish Apocrypha, and Christian scripture – canonical and apocryphal. The particular texts and passages have been selected by virtue of their contribution, either to the formation of a central biblical 'manifesto', that is, the construction of the notion of a divinely ordered universe overseen through omnipotence, or to an anarchic counter-culture – usually manifested through divine collusion.

Inevitably, selecting biblical texts for analysis attracts criticism from reviewers and readers regarding the choice of texts and the bias evident in that choice. The texts I have selected include a variety of literary types: narrative, law, poetry and letters. Though diverse in terms of type and historical setting, these texts all display a common interest in power, both divine and human, and how it functions – and how it might be destabilised. The cycles of devastation and hope that characterise Hebrew scriptures offer a theological pattern that is replicated and effective in shaping both Judaism and Christianity. Walter Brueggemann has pointed out how the experience of exile – so significant in the formulation and shaping of Hebrew scripture – had an ongoing influence:

> The exile as event, experience, memory, and paradigm looms large over the literature and faith of the Old Testament. Together with the restoration, the exile emerged as the decisive reference point for the self-understanding of Judaism. Moreover, the power of the exile and restoration

2

as an imaginative construct exercised enormous impact on subsequent Christian understandings of faith and life as they were recast in terms of crucifixion and resurrection.

(1992: 183)

The influence and significance of such a pattern stands as a challenge to biblical scholars to broaden their critical lens outwards from the minutiae of pericopes and to examine the wider context – the theological stances and world-views – that motivated and framed the thinking of biblical authors. The breadth of this study, embracing texts from the Hebrew Bible and Christian scripture does not reflect a confessional stance, but rather a hermeneutical one. In order to understand the framework of early Christian writings, it is vital to understand theologies of the texts that were at the forefront of the religious experience of their writers. Likewise, apocryphal and early Christian writings stand as examples of how Hebrew scriptures were understood and applied in the first century CE – a time a lot closer to their origin than our own! The themes and ideas informing these apocryphal and Christian writers offer us a hermeneutical window onto the theological arena of earlier centuries – particularly in terms of the nature of God and the relationship between God and humanity.

The context of postmodernity has allowed the fragmentary nature of western/colonial culture to be exposed through processes of deconstruction applied to myriad sites within the multi-layered metanarrative of 'western civilisation'. If that context and its analysis can be understood in, albeit fragmenting, macrocosmic terms, then the Bible can represent a reflective microcosm – one that has been subjected to similar monolithic readings, but can be deconstructed to reveal a pluralistic tension of institutions, practices and discourses that coexist in the metanarrative of a canon of scripture that conflicts and negates within itself. The 'accident' of the particular set of texts we call the Bible – whether the Jewish or Christian version, or the Catholic or Protestant one – can be explained in many ways. In confessional contexts particular collections of biblical material are believed to be the product of divine selectivity – brought about with more or less divine intervention depending on the nature of the belief system of a faith community. Rather than take a radical postmodern critical stance and see our various Bibles as ad hoc accidental collections, through this study I would suggest that there is evidence of a consistent subjective agency that manifests itself, in differing shapes and forms, as divine omnipotence. This is articulated in

3

response to particular manifestations within the ancient biblical worlds of political superpowers with supremacy relative to narrow and broad world-views of the various times. Thus, although there is a notion of a consistent biblical agency, the form it takes is contingent upon the context of the faith community – the author/editor/ reader – that is imaging resistance. Therefore, the explanation for the existence of the various collections that form biblical texts – the work of the myriad authors and editors – is ultimately self-interest. The communities that selected the texts that come under the generic term 'biblical' shared a common characteristic: disillusionment – with world order and with the ancient concept of a 'superpower', whether it be Assyrian, Babylonian, Persian, Hellenistic or Roman. The divine agency necessarily mutates to resist these forces, and to defeat them, if only in microcosmic situations rather than in the hoped-for macrocosmic cosmological sense (see Aberbach 1993). A recent study by Mark Brett presents the book of Genesis against the backcloth of Persian imperialism – the context for the text's final editing – and in doing so uncovers the complexity of an 'intentional hybridity' (2000: 22), a term he borrows from Mikhail Bakhtin (1981: 358–61), that offers an explanation for the tensions in the text that, in themselves, in their 'unstable chorale', present resistance to the dominant Persian colonial power:

> In the case of Genesis, the overriding ideologies have been juxtaposed with so many traces of otherness that the dominant voices can be deconstructed by those who have ears to hear.
>
> (Brett 2000: 22)

The present study includes biblical texts that stem from a variety of colonial contexts in the ancient world, and suggests that, collectively, they can be understood in terms of a 'new essentialism' for biblical theology. This is a hermeneutical stance borrowed from contemporary gender theory that deconstructs the phenomenon 'woman' as the constructed 'other' and presents possibilities for reconstructing woman subjectively, as exemplified in the work of Luce Irigaray (see Schor and Weed 1994). Woman can become woman through and of herself, as opposed to what is 'other' to male identity. Biblical theologies have been constantly produced to reflect dominant belief systems throughout history, where images of God have been carefully selected to reflect the prevailing notions of power. The biblical 'gods' have not simply emerged down the ages 'through and of' the many and diverse accounts of divine actions described in the texts. Mirroring the emergence of Irigaray's 'new' woman, the biblical God can shine through in his myriad moods and guises. But this is contingent upon whether the inconsistencies of his many portrayals are allowed to exist side by side rather than be subjected to exegesis intent on producing a monolithic meaning (Brueggemann 1997).

A 'new essentialist' approach to biblical texts is essentialist in presuming that a biblical metanarrative runs through the various 'bibles', and 'new' in that it realistically assesses the relativism of biblical texts. Thus the metanarrative that emerges is clearly marked with the relative values of past cultures and value systems rather than overlaid with contemporary ones. Any attempt to apply biblical notions to the contemporary world can only be authentic if it is informed by a knowledge of past worlds and not a selected past peered at through the narrow telescopic lens of Christian or Jewish heritage. Of course, all renderings of history are selective and subjective, but even the acknowledgement of this truism is a step forward for biblical studies – a field that has sadly lacked the discipline of self-awareness, a lack encapsulated in its naive post-Enlightenment project of objective historical criticism.

To use Gadamer's term, the *Wirkungsgeschichte* of biblical texts – the history of their effectiveness or impact – can be monitored down the centuries, marked, particularly in the context of Christian exegesis, by intensifying patriarchal assertion. Prescribed meaning modifies and changes to reflect given political realities of the time and, as the meaning modifies, so the text's impact shifts and challenges its socio-political contexts anew. This hermeneutical circle explains how meaning and experience are inseparable and unstable, and awareness of it exposes the quest for objective meaning as a post-Enlightenment myth. Historical critical research has dominated biblical studies in the modern period. The enterprise to search for the original meaning of sacred texts has had a plurality of motives, ranging from Reimarus' clumsy attempts to disprove the resurrection and miracle narratives of the Gospels in the name of the superiority of human reason over primitive superstition, to the invention of so-called 'scientific criteria' by Christian pastors in academic guise in their quest for the historical Jesus. Not surprisingly, this Jesus usually turns out to be the mirror image of the liberal Protestants who seek him out – with slight modifications depending on time and context. The severe gaze of these critics becomes blind to the biases of their own times, as though modernity exists in a sterile vacuum:

5

> Moreover, historical criticism has implicitly veiled the historical character of biblical scholarship's entanglements with modernity and has therefore left unexamined its own critical and theoretical assumptions as well as the cultural conditions that produced, sustained, and validated them.
>
> (Aichele *et al.* 1995: 2)

Other trends in contemporary biblical scholarship acknowledge the value of biases and openly declare them from the outset, and this is illustrated most clearly in the work of liberation and feminist theologians. These theologians, in pursuing their own clearly identified political agendas, added a vital force in the demolition work of deconstruction in the context of biblical academia. In questioning the point, or even the possibility, of achieving an unbiased reading they joined forces with the cultural mood of postmodernity.

The field of present-day biblical studies holds a unique position in the academy. As a product of the modernity project itself, with its origins stemming from the Reformation, it exists as an enigma. It is an academic subject that has parodied itself through its quest for objective meaning, and yet this quest is executed by scholars who are either confessing Christians, in a line of tradition from the 'fathers' of the Reformation to Bultmann and his generation, and beyond to new misguided quests for the 'historical truth' of two millennia ago, or zealous non-believers, or ex-believers, following in the footsteps of their forefather Reimarus. Biblical ideas on all aspects of human identity and existence that are mediated by such scholarship belong within the confines of Christian theology, most notably of the western liberal Protestant variety, and offer only a limited contribution to contemporary studies of antiquity.

Many scholars in the past half-century have divulged the damage that has been caused to Jewish studies by supersessionist Christian biblical scholarship and they have identified the endemic, sinister presence of anti-Semitism in the biblical academy (Klein 1975; Plaskow 1994). Sadly, the tendency to negate Judaism by naming it as Christianity's 'other' in order to affirm the truth of the latter was evident in academic departments of theology and biblical studies, as well as in more overtly Christian contexts. Biblical studies and Christian 'faith' agendas have an incestuous relationship, and the presence of the former in the academy has allowed the fallacy of objectivity to be promulgated in the most incongruous circumstances. The impetus and result of any scholarly search for the 'real' meaning of a passage of scripture have ultimate implications for a confessional rather than an academic audience. To discover what St Paul actually meant when he exhorted women to cover their heads has implications for worshipping women, not secular feminists. Biblical studies can never form an objective academic exercise – whatever that might be. It has existed as an effective white, western/ colonial, patriarchal discourse – a microcosmic affirmation of western culture. When biblical studies are executed in a postmodern climate, they are immediately liberated from the impetus to discover an objective meaning inevitably measured in Christian theological terms. The plurality of meanings and values that characterise post-modernity transpose biblical texts from such constraints to a variety of contexts in academia and wider culture.

Any study that attempts to analyse the notion of God and his relationship with humanity as it is expressed within biblical litera-ture has to take account of the divinely ordained roles described in the Bible for men and women. These both reflect on the nature of the God who has ordained them and, ironically, offer possibilities for divine action to break through and disrupt them. For two millennia, when questions have arisen regarding the appropriate roles for men and women, Jewish and Christian commentators have had recourse to sacred texts, many of which they share. It is assumed that the explanation of the origin and cause for the differences between men and women is contained within these sacred texts. Furthermore, their sacred nature ensures the authority and veracity of the explanation. The text is the root and sustenance of subsequent belief and understanding. In Judaism, God's Torah – both written and oral – pre-exists the creation of humanity and anticipates all subsequent experience; and, likewise, in Christian belief the Bible contains the totality of God's intention for humanity and the world. In these religious contexts the text pre-empts all existence – any space we might think to negotiate has already been anticipated and occupied. All-encompassing, the alpha and omega, sacred text serves as a metanarrative, and the power of the divine λογος spans the entire cosmos:

> In the beginning was the λογος, and the λογος was with God, and the λογος was God. It was in the beginning with God. All things came into being through it, and without it not one thing came into being.
>
> (John 1.1–3)

In biblical terms there is no human experience before Adam and Eve, and it is their creation and dialogue with the creator that produces the blueprint for male and female identity and behaviour categories. To conceive of these categories being constructed phenomena is inappropriate in theological contexts. One construction can imply the possibility of alternatives, or even the possibility of chance and accident, rather than a foundational piece of an omniscient plan.

Taken out of a theological environment, the Genesis account of the origin and cause of human existence can itself be identified as product of a particular society at a particular moment in history. In the context of postmodernity, theories of myth and methods of deconstruction reveal the paradise episode as a commentary – a reflection – on the particular society that produced it. This switches the sacred text from its theological position as universal metatruth, to a particular context, and it becomes one of many cultural commentaries in a fragmented world. Contemporary interest in the nature of the ancient society that produced the biblical creation story is matched by commentators who look back at the story's history of interpretation – how it has shaped, and how its meaning has been shaped by, western and colonial political and social interests.

Michel Foucault's genealogical critique allows power relations to be explored by an analysis of the dominant discourse operating at a particular period of time in conflict with competing discourses:

> We must not imagine a world of discourse divided between accepted discourse and excluded discourse, or between the dominant discourse and the dominated one; but as a multiplicity of discursive elements that can come into play in various strategies.
>
> (1984: 100)

Following Foucault, but extending his theory to include gender analysis, the contemporary philosopher Judith Butler reveals gender categories as political formulations rather than essential markers of identity. Rather than search for the origin of male and female gender, Butler sees the pragmatic project to be more one that destabilises the notion of gender itself, since it is a construction and regulation of identity:

> Genealogy investigates the political stakes in designating as an *origin* and *cause* those identity categories that are in

fact the *effects* of institutions, practices, discourses with multiple and diffuse points of origin.

(1990: ix)

Instead of understanding identity categories ontologically (primarily, as binary masculine and feminine gender underpinned with compulsory heterosexuality) and as informing and formulating particular socio-political contexts, they are, in fact, the *products* of those contexts. Clearly, the Bible, in both religious and cultural terms, can be understood as such a discourse par excellence that has *effected* – constructed – identity categories. But, as Butler points out, the institutions, practices and discourses that construct identity are themselves multiple and diffuse with their own histories.

The possibility that, within the Bible, one unchanging meta-discourse might exist has been a common illusion in modernity as well as pre-modernity. The unselfconscious common belief held by Christianity, from the time of late antiquity, that the biblical canon contained divine revelation that, by its nature, could not be contradictory or fallible, continues in many faith contexts today. In more recent times, German scholars claimed to have uncovered the unifying discourse of *Heilsgeschichte*, 'salvation history', whereas liberation and feminist theologians divulged the consistent liberation motif with a divine option for the oppressed and marginalised. The existence of a multiplicity of biblical metareadings testifies to the multiplicity of biblical discourses, and these discourses have their own prehistory, and impact history. This multiplicity has been dealt with by the 'metareaders' through the process of silencing – by the non-reading of texts that fall outside a current ideology. Once cut free of the imperative to fit biblical meaning into a monolithic discourse, the text cascades into a profusion of ideas and concepts that can be met by a myriad of meanings. Not only are we challenged to find unambiguous definitions of what essentially constitutes a man or a woman, but biblical concepts of human identity and autonomy can be displayed across a wide spectrum – from eternal infantile dependency to the ultimate power of sovereignty.

The breadth of diversity of writers and audiences embraced within the biblical parameters is awesome, and yet, at various times in the history of the evolution of the text as well as its transmission, single-minded editors/authors have attempted to imprint a particular discourse onto their texts or collections of texts. These discourses reflect the prevailing imperial and patriarchal interests – even in their resistance to alien regimes the power represented by them, although displaced, is replicated. Certainly, particular empires differ in terms of their time and space, just as patriarchies exist on various levels of intensity, and yet these variables do not preclude an essential shared characteristic of desire for absolute power, however liberally or ruthlessly managed, in the hands of men, however benevolent or misogynist in their treatment of women. These essentialist features of ancient political reality are all reflected in the biblical portrayals of the divine. Whilst wishing to display and celebrate the breadth and diversity of biblical images of the divine and the human – male and female – and the multitude of relations existing within this eternal triangle, there is a discernible intensification of a particular paradigm. This intensification occurs in harmony with political developments in the ancient world. As power becomes more concentrated in fewer centres of control, so the omnipotence of the divine becomes more uncompromisingly absolute – the emergence of bigger empires and their accompanying emperors is mirrored by a monotheistic, theocratic theology. The demands placed on the adherents to this divinity become total in recognition of the nature of absolute power, rivalling any allegiance of subjects within an empire. The uncovering and exploration of these features as they are played out in the divine/human relations depicted in biblical literature across the centuries form the main subject of this volume.

The Bible contains varieties of constructions of gender that compete and contradict across the breadth of the canon, and we will be exploring this rich collection in the coming chapters. But as the question of human identity is more deeply explored it becomes evident that one of the most consistent, recurrent biblical images of humanity is that of being infantile. Correspondingly, the pervading biblical divine image is that of parent, almost invariably that of father.

The fatherhood of the biblical God is a relatively neglected theme in studies of Hebrew scriptures; usually it is reserved for scholars of Christian scripture who identify it as the distinctive feature of Jesus of Nazareth's theology (see Chapter 6). It is true that, in Hebrew scriptures, the word 'father' (אב) rarely appears as a form of address for God (see Deut. 32.6; Isa. 63.16, 64.8), nor is it frequently used by God to describe his relationship with his people. This does not mean, however, that the notion of the fatherhood of God is barely present in those scriptures. Katheryn Pfisterer Darr's study of familial imagery in Isaiah clearly illustrates this observation (1994: 46–84). A key image in descriptions of the elect nation's relationship with God is that of sonship (for example, Exod. 4.22; Deut.

14.1; Isa. 1.2, 45.11; Jer. 3.19; Hos. 11.1; and Mal. 2.10). If the 'male' God of these scriptures addresses Israel as his 'son', surely it is not out of harmony with this language and imagery then to perceive of God as 'father'? In the examples mentioned, it is important to note how often this familial imagery is linked to God's creative activity, thus suggesting the image of God as the father of the first couple (see Chapter 2).

It is surprising how scholars have neglected teasing out the implications of biblical writers employing this familial imagery. Maybe because most biblical scholars were fathers themselves, living in eras where models of fatherhood were given, accepted and followed uncritically, this image and, more importantly, its interpretation were assumed. Late twentieth-century feminist critique of patriarchy, particularly its deconstruction, has opened up the image of fatherhood for examination and, in the wider context of postmodernity, new and alternative interpretations coexist alongside the 'traditional'. Rather than assuming that the images of father, parent and child form an unchanging paradigm in human existence and experience, the realisation of the relativity of meaning of these relations allows their depiction in the ancient biblical world to be more vividly understood.

Following in the footsteps of liberation theologians, feminist biblical scholars have allowed pre-eminence to biblical texts that advocate inclusion of the marginalised and liberation for the oppressed in an era when western culture has, at least partially, embraced forms of 'political correctness' and aspects of a feminist agenda. Phyllis Trible and Elisabeth Schüssler Fiorenza, working on the Hebrew and Christian scriptures respectively and employing diverse methodologies, are two notable figures who share the hermeneutical stance of feminism in their aim to uncover positive attitudes to women in the Bible. Their scholarship is characteristic of second-wave feminism, itself inspired by political feminism of the 1960s and 1970s that focused on patriarchy as the essential characteristic of western society, culture and politics. Simone de Beauvoir's classic analysis, *The Second Sex*, divulged woman as the 'other' whose existence upholds the authenticity and supremacy of male ascendancy, while feminist biblical scholars named the many biblical texts that collude and enable patriarchal systems through the type of relationships depicted between God and human beings, and between men and women. Examples include the Genesis narratives; the legislation in Leviticus; the Household Codes in Colossians, Ephesians and 1 Peter; the silencing of women in the Pastoral Epistles; and accounts of the victims of patriarchy, including abused women (Judg. 19), and abused children (Gen. 22). Such texts have been exposed as exceptions to the biblical theme of liberation and excluded from the 'feminist canon' (Ruether 1985; Fiorenza 1994). Conversely, texts that appear to challenge patriarchy and infer its reform, if not its end – texts that can be read almost as parodies of traditional gender polarisations of masculine and feminine pre-scribed behaviour – become the new canon, having been processed by feminist hermeneutics. Included among these texts are the account of Tamar in Genesis 38; the book of Ruth; the story of the Samaritan woman in John's Gospel; the women activists in the early urban Christian communities mentioned by St Paul; and, par excellence, Galatians 3.28. The need to search out a 'canon within the canon', evident down the centuries, but distinctly prevalent in a variety of contemporary contexts, is commented on by George Aichele in his recent reappraisal of the notion of 'canon' (2001: 96). In analysing these texts of the feminist 'canon' in this volume, I will be asking if the central role these texts have had in shaping contem-porary feminist theology has restricted the scope of the feminist hermeneutical project. To understand power and patriarchy in the Bible a wider lens is needed, and focusing primarily on selected biblical women distorts the picture. The manner in which mascu-linity is presented is an additional vital issue and, of course, so is the nature of the deity.

While it can be clearly understood why feminist biblical and theo-logical scholarship has clustered around particular texts, this has worked to restrict the scope of contemporary feminist theology and, at times, has blinded it from asking more searching questions as to why certain texts do in fact challenge the boundaries. Phyllis Trible describes a 'depatriarchalized' Bible (1973) that presumes an acultural level of existence for biblical texts – or, rather, certain texts. There is a level of meaning, according to Trible, that tran-scends the culture in which it was produced, and in which it was transmitted. This level of meaning lies in a space that can only exist, can only be explained, at the level of faith. It is contingent on the reader's particular situation within a community of faith, and in that acknowledged space it is a reality, but obviously not a universal one. For those outside the community of faith there can be no 'depatriarchalised' Bible – however large or small that imag-ined text might be. When we stand outside that community of reformist feminist believers and ask why these texts confront patri-archal boundaries, we may not conclude with Trible that they are the challenge of a 'depatriarchalised' god, but rather that they are the ultimate finesse of a very patriarchal god.

The essentially patriarchal nature of biblical texts has long been identified, although opinion still divides on the question of what might be recovered or 'depatriarchalised' for those with a reformist feminist theological agenda. Feminist critique has uncovered many examples of narratives in which biblical writers have employed female characters for pragmatic purposes – often to underline the omniscient power of the deity. In narratives that allow pre-eminence to particular women, male characters can be denigrated to positions of powerlessness. In the biblical context, where male supremacy is assumed, this process of emasculation functions to destabilise the audience's expectations, and allows the author to apply the surprise tactic of a male deity using female vehicles to ensure his plan is accomplished. Narratives employing this tactic include the accounts of Sarah, Hagar and Abraham; Rebecca and Isaac; Rachel and Jacob; Tamar and Judah; and Naomi, Ruth and Boaz. Also, this theme carries on into the apocryphal literature, presenting us with the supreme example of Judith and Holofernes, and is discernible in early Christian texts, where the male disciples are outshone by the faith of the women around Jesus. Even – or especially – the account of the first couple in paradise allows for such a reading. Biblical scholars have revealed how the recurring theme of overturning primogeniture characterises the story of Genesis, and this process is usually abetted by female collusion. Furthermore, these consistent key moments of female empowerment characterise not only Genesis, but also stories throughout the Jewish and Christian canons and apocryphal texts.

When contemporary gender theory is applied to this particular theme within biblical literature, it becomes evident that both masculinity and femininity have been destabilised within the patriarchal framework, and not with the intention to undermine this world-view, but rather to reinforce it. The supreme manifestation of patriarchy – the power of the male god – is triumphant and remains assured. Mere male mortals can be ridiculed in this scheme in the service of this higher purpose. Judith Butler has argued that subversion of given gender roles is consistently evident within patriarchy, and she takes these exceptions to demonstrate the fragility of constructed gender:

> If the inner truth of gender is a fabrication and if a true
> gender is a fantasy instituted and inscribed on the surface

of bodies, then it seems that genders can be neither true nor false, but are only produced as the truth effects of a discourse of primary and stable identity.

(Butler 1990: 136)

Such fragility of the given behaviour patterns is clearly apparent in biblical narrative, whatever theological purpose may be served by it. The biblical law codes reflect an uncompromising construction of prescribed gendered behaviour, and set beside them are narratives that subvert them. In this alternative scenario, as Butler writes, the reality of plurality can be recognised:

> Cultural configurations of sex and gender might then proliferate or, rather, their present proliferation might then become articulable within the discourses that establish intelligible cultural life, confounding the very binarism of sex, and exposing its fundamental unnaturalness.
>
> (1990: 149)

But there is a lack of reality to existence 'outside' constructed space. Any space has to be negotiated within existing socio-political realities and, by the very act of negotiating, an engagement occurs and one identity becomes subsumed by another. Butler's concept of performative gender expressed in *Gender Trouble* was criticised for not taking into account the realities of enforced identity through race – and the accompanying dominant white liberal humanist discourse – as well as gender. In Butler's eyes such criticism is a misreading of her ideas that, she argues, do offer a way forward for identities to shift, but not at the expense of the negation of others:

> If through its own violences, the conceits of liberal humanism have compelled the multiplication of culturally specific identities, then it is all the more important not to repeat that violence without a significant difference, reflexively and prescriptively, within the articulatory struggles of those specific identities forged from and through a state of seige. That identifications shift does not necessarily mean that one identification is repudiated for another; that shifting may well be one sign of hope for the possibility of avowing an expansive set of connections.
>
> (1993: 118)

The option of performative identity remains an unreality for the majority who cannot grasp at a vision of life beyond their constructed reality. But this criticism of Butler is suspended when the scene of the performance is something beyond human controlled space. Butler's performative identity theory is the ideal tool to apply to biblical texts where the central characters *can* defy and escape constructed realities.

Contemporary gender theoretician Luce Irigaray's use of 'mimesis' (*mimétisme*) in exploring female subjectivity, where authenticity might lie more in the *parody* of objectified womanhood than in the male constructed model, also resonates with the gender games apparent in biblical narratives. Although often labelled as 'new essentialism' (see above, pp. 4–5), the very nature of Irigaray's work defies any attempt at a static categorisation. Her thought is constantly fluid, often representing a multiplicity of positions: 'Irigaray means for us to understand everything she says as "double-voiced". Or triple or quadruple . . . multiple' (Weir 1996: 96). Through her application of the concept of mimesis, Irigaray attempts to transform the notion of 'woman'. This is achieved by deconstructing the patriarchal construct of woman as 'other' to man and allowing for the possibility of woman to emerge from within that difference, to be 'herself' for the first time: 'One must assume the feminine role deliberately. Which means already to convert a form of subordination into an affirmation, and thus to begin to thwart it' (Irigaray 1985: 76). Irigaray's use of mimesis 'imitation' – her parody of the constructed notion of woman – allows for the appropriation of femininity with the female as subject: 'To play with mimesis is thus, for a woman, to try to recover the place of her exploitation by discourse, without allowing herself to be simply reduced to it' (1985: 76).

Irigaray works with the notion of difference, and proposes a new essentialism that is both individual and independent of the masculine 'other'. In the biblical world, maleness and masculinity are constructed as the 'other' to God. Applying Irigaray's notion of mimesis to biblical manhood could suggest new ways of reading biblical texts that impact on both male and female images. For example, the image of an active Adam who takes and eats the forbidden fruit in order to gain autonomy can emerge, in contrast to the image of Adam as the reluctant victim of Eve's temptation. The gender games apparent in biblical literature apply as much to constructed masculinity as to femininity. However, through focusing primarily on female characters in biblical literature, feminist critique has often overlooked the implications of constructed masculinity.

The analysis of gender construction is vital to understanding the way in which the themes of biblical texts often interact with one another within the canon – given gender behavioural patterns in one text are challenged in another. But gender roles are enacted by the secondary characters in the major plot. The one main character remains in place throughout biblical narrative, often wearing different guises within or outside gendered boundaries – sometimes even cross-dressing – but always steering the plot and being served by the supporting cast. While it is important to analyse human biblical characters – the minor players – in order to understand the plot, and to gain insights into the main character, to over-invest in their significance is to lose sight of the grand narrative. In the biblical literature these secondary characters with their stories always remain shadows, reflecting a diminished divine glory.

The Bible as sacred text contains within it three categories relevant to our analysis: texts that can be seen clearly to be in harmony with a hierarchical and patriarchal society; texts that challenge, subvert and infer the reformation of such a society; and texts that can be read in anarchic terms totally overturning expected societal norms. This explicit tension present in any one canon of scripture that attempts to hold these texts as one is a phenomenon that Walter Brueggemann has recognised in relation to the Hebrew scriptures. He encourages scholars to work with this tension, which is the essential characteristic of biblical theology, rather than attempt to resolve it:

> A careful understanding of the literature shows that we are *not free to resolve* the tension. The Old Testament both partakes of the common theology and struggles to be free from it. The Old Testament both enters the fray of ambiguity and seeks distance from the fray to find something certain and sure. The God of Israel is thus presented variously as the God above the fray who appears like other Near Eastern gods and as a God who is exposed in the fray, who appears unlike the gods of common theology, a God peculiarly available for Israel's historical experiences.
>
> (1992: 5)

His characterisation of the 'Old Testament' can be equally valid for the Christian canon. In order to examine this tension across a broad spectrum of biblical literature, I have used the apparent contradictions as a means of providing the structure for the remainder of this study, beginning with the next chapter, entitled 'Setting the Boundaries', where I discuss texts that present the biblical world-view/s and value system/s. In the third chapter, 'Testing the Boundaries', I discuss how these set boundaries are challenged in order to ensure that God's plan for the destiny of Israel is fulfilled. In the fourth chapter, 'Breaking the Boundaries', I show how this paradoxical theme, which presents humanity with boundaries that are then blown apart by divine behaviour, intensifies in the books of Judges and Ruth — a trend particularly apparent through the ways in which female characters are portrayed. In the fifth chapter, 'Crossing the Boundaries', I discuss how biblical writers — active within the context of the greater-than-ever superpowers of the ancient world — employ gender as a literary strategy in a theological enterprise. This strategy involves both female and male characters where the elevation of the former is closely paralleled by the emasculation of the latter. The primary material for the fifth chapter also crosses canonical boundaries, moving from the Hebrew Bible to the Jewish Apocrypha, and then to the Christian Gospels. The sixth chapter, 'Reconfiguring the Boundaries', continues to explore the significance of the context of the Roman Empire for informing early Christian notions of power, and for understanding the familial language consistently employed by first- and second-century writers that is then reconfigured in relation to God and emerging patterns of belief. The final chapter, 'Last Things', focuses on examples of anarchic biblical imagery that unsettle and challenge order and expectation. Here, again, gender is used strategically, effectively illustrating how an ordered hierarchy can be turned upside down when the Creator decides to exercise his unique power. In the last section I suggest how the anarchic strand in biblical literature can offer alternative paradigms for our own times through scenes and characters that challenge the lack of autonomy in the dominant biblical paradigm for the divine/human relationship.

2

SETTING THE
BOUNDARIES

CREATION

> The naming is at once the setting of a boundary, and also the
> repeated inculcation of a norm.
>
> (Butler 1993: 8)

The Genesis story of Adam and Eve encapsulates the tension between
the two ways of being human in relation to God – the choice
between obedience and autonomy. This foundation text for the
biblical discourse explains that God created the heavens and the
earth and all that is in them, and arranged things in order, with
the human species in control but subjugated to divine omnipotence.
The first time human beings are mentioned in the biblical text is
in relation to God:

> Then God said, 'Let us make humankind in our image,
> according to our likeness; and let them have dominion over
> the fish of the sea, and over the birds of the air, and over
> the cattle, and over all the wild animals of the earth, and
> over every creeping thing that creeps upon the earth.'
>
> (Gen. 1.26)

Human beings are to be brought into being by the will of God, and
they are to be in the image of God, in the likeness of God.
Furthermore, their primary characteristic is to emulate the power
of God in their domination of all living creatures: birds, fish,
domestic animals and even insects. From the very beginning,
arguing from the sequence in Genesis 1.26, the essential human
characteristic, according to the Bible, is the ability, conjoined with
the imperative, to imitate God. The concept of bearing the image

18

of God is given form, made manifest, through the visible exercise of human power within the created order. Furthermore, within the created order there exists a gendered human hierarchy, described in Genesis 2.

The belief about the nature of humanity conveyed by Genesis 1.26 has had a formative impact on western and colonial ideas and culture, making it one of the most influential and interpreted verses in literature. From antiquity to medieval times, from the Reformation period to the Enlightenment, and from modernity to postmodernity, and with readings ranging from Jewish to Christian, literal to allegorical, Protestant to Catholic, liberationist to feminist, the idea of manifesting the image of God still captivates the human imagination. This fascination itself divulges the inherent power recognised in the concept of *imago dei*.

In one of the most significant books in postmodern biblical scholarship, Elizabeth Castelli explores the concept of mimesis as it relates to the theology of Paul of Tarsus (1991). In particular, she identifies and explores the concept of power in a relationship characterised by mimesis, where Paul exhorts his communities to imitate him, as he, in turn, imitates Christ: 'Be imitators of me, as I am of Christ' (μιμηται μου γινεσθε, καθως καγω Χριστου) (1 Cor. 11.1; see also 1 Cor. 4.16; Phil. 3.17, 4.9; 1 Thess. 1.6–7). Castelli does not link the concepts of mimesis and image – *imitatio dei/christi* with *imago dei*. This might reflect a 'static' understanding of the latter, in contrast to the 'active' concept of imitating – more resonant with classical parallels. Or, more probably, such a connection is not obvious because the link between *imago dei* and the verb to subjugate – רדה – made in the same divine utterance (Gen. 1.26) suggests an empowered imitator rather than the disempowered subject drawn by Castelli's deconstruction of *imitatio dei*:

> imitation implies . . . a critical relationship of power, insofar as the model represents the standard toward which its copies move. The model sets the terms of the relationship, which is both hierarchical and asymmetrical.
>
> (1991: 22)

The concept of *imago dei* set up in Genesis 1.26 constructs a multi-stratified hierarchy with absolute power at the pinnacle, and a recognisable but diminished power in its human reflection. Although limited, the power of that reflection is affirmed by the subjection of the lower strata that range from mammals to insect life. *Imago dei* could well lie behind the Pauline concept of *imitatio dei/christi* – in essence, both serve to reinforce the status of the blueprint. This structure opening the biblical narrative becomes its matrix and is endorsed and developed by Christian writers and thinkers. Their contribution will be discussed more fully in Chapter 6.

The privileging of human beings by virtue of the *imago dei* does not have to imply their equality with their maker or indeed their deification. Their subjectivity in the presence of the divine creator is constantly asserted in the text. The tree 'in the midst of the Garden' might hold the secret of godliness, but that has been expressly forbidden to humanity. The information Eve receives from the serpent is flawed: 'You will not die; for God knows that when you eat of it your eyes will be opened, and you will be like gods, knowing good and evil' (Gen. 3.4–5). In fact they do die, and they never achieve likeness to the divine in regard of any equality of power. Moral discernment would seem to be the only prize available – one that introduces them to the harsh reality of the adult, uniquely human world. Making decisions on the basis of a moral judgement distinguishes human beings from the animal kingdom and, significantly, takes human beings out of the state of perpetual childhood under the parenthood of God. If this is the godlike quality that humanity possesses (snatched rather than bestowed – the antithesis of the 'kenotic' process described by Paul in Phil. 2.6–8), then the distinction between humanity 'inside the Garden' and 'outside' is one of autonomy, or becoming adult (see York 1996; Rudman 2001). Alicia Ostriker succinctly and poetically describes the unreality of human existence in paradise:

> Something is still missing. For their brains, those ripening walnuts, are as wide as the sky but also as blank as clouds. Forming, flowing, diffuse, changing and lovely, their minds retain no shape, have need of none. No need of an identity, or a memory, they to whom the world is an omnipresent nipple.
>
> (1994: 22)

Jewish commentators suggest that the biblical narrative describing the creation of human beings is complete only in Genesis 3 when free will is recognised as a crucial element in human existence as it faces up to the realities of life – work, pain, violence and difficult relationships. Rabbi Akiba neatly sums up the eternal paradox for humanity living within the biblical boundaries: 'Everything is seen and freedom of choice is given' (Mishnah *Avoth* 3.25). Adam and Eve leave the playground of Eden to become human, and the story of their creation is completed. Free will could not be 'created into' human existence – it had to be freely taken. In effect, God had to trick human beings into 'taking' free will through an emissary – the serpent. The twentieth-century Christian theologian Karl Barth sees the action of taking the forbidden fruit as symptomatic of human pride that estranges humanity from God, and he emphasises the neutral role played by the serpent which simply articulates the alternative to the divine command (Barth 1956: 420–1). Eve is presented with a choice, and in choosing to possess the ability to discern between good and evil, the decision is made to take on autonomy.

A central Christian tradition, evident in patristic, medieval and reformation theology, understands Eve's action as the 'fall' with cosmic implications, and the serpent becomes the devil in reptilian disguise. In this tradition it is asserted that humanity, and nature, lost its perfection and was now maimed as a consequence of this act of disobedience. There is no gain to human existence through this action, instead something is apparently lost, and this is articulated in terms of a diminished possession of the divine image. According to the Christian doctrine of original sin, this 'fall' for the Bible's first couple results in a particular estrangement from God for all subsequent humanity. This blemished human nature is passed on through the generations, according to Augustine of Hippo, via sexual intercourse, and is a constant essential characteristic of 'fallen' humanity (*Literal Meaning of Genesis* XI: 32). The only 'cure' for this condition is the grace of God, and the only exceptions from the infection are the Son of God and his mother who experienced immaculate conceptions. When the story of Adam and Eve is read in the context of traditional Christian theology, the emphasis is placed on the estrangement from God – the expulsion from the Garden. For Christians this is the first instalment of the story of redemption: the ideal, perfect relationship between God and humanity, prefigured but never realised until the time of its manifestation through the person of Jesus Christ. Paradoxically, the act of disobedience becomes a sign of hope, poignantly expressed in a fifteenth-century anonymous poem:

> Ne had the apple taken been
> The apple taken been,
> Ne hadde never our Lady
> A been heaven's queen.
> Blessed be the time

That apple taken was!
Therefore we may singen
'Deo Gratias!'

(Gardner 1972: 13–14)

The ideal relationship that is subsequently described in Christian scripture between God and Christ is characterised as that of parent and child. Free will, in Christian terms, is rejected in favour of radical dependence on God.

It can be argued that the traditional Christian reading is more consonant with the text than the positivist interpretation that recognises the taking of the fruit as the first step towards full and mature humanity. Throughout subsequent biblical narrative a consistent desire to return to the prelapsarian childlike state is voiced, despite this condition being characterised by lack of autonomy – a theme identified in Darr's study of Isaiah's utopian imagery: 'Present suffering notwithstanding, God offers repentant Israel a world so edenic, so devoid of natural calamity and human strife, that even its curious toddlers cannot get into trouble' (1994: 83). This theme exists in tension with the alternative, less pervasive, biblical current that encourages human discernment.

The Bible's opening chapters explain how human life, and all of creation, is dependent on the Creator for its existence. The first story, as it is presented in the canons edited and shaped by generations of ideas and experiences, provides clear indications of the power structures between God, human beings, living creatures and nature. God's supremacy, as Creator, over the world is self-evident, but it is affirmed by further actions in the opening scenes: the creation, subjection and domination of all living creatures – this is the boundary of the human domain. They are drawn and given by God, demonstrating that God is the source of all human power. Through imitation, human beings, created in God's image, share the power characteristics: subjection and domination of all living creatures. What they do not share, what they cannot imitate, is the work of creation – here they are subject to divine omnipotence like the rest of creation. Paradoxically, through imaging the divine, humanity is destined always to be less than gods:

What are human beings that you
are mindful of them,
mortals (בן אדם) that you care for
them?

22

Yet you have made them a little
lower than God (אלהים),
and crowned them with glory
and honour.
You have given them dominion
over the works of your
hands;
you have put all things under
their feet,
all sheep and oxen,
and also the beasts of the field,
the birds of the air and the fish
of the sea . . .

O Lord, our Sovereign,
how majestic is your name in all
the earth!

(Ps. 8.4–9)

These verses from the Psalmist reflect both the status of and also
the limits for humanity, which bears the likeness of the Creator, but
which is essentially subordinate to divine omnipotence.

When the Genesis narrative comes to describe in more detail
the creation of gendered humanity, we can observe a patterning of
dependency. Adam, or man, is created first: moulded into shape
by the hands of God, and given the breath of life by the mouth of
God. But God recognises that Adam has no partner, no likeness.
Before creating Eve, God creates all the rest of the living creatures,
parading them in front of Adam, and Adam exercises his authority
over them by naming them. But there is no creature that adequately
reflects his likeness – no creature that can be his partner and
helper (Gen. 2.20). When God does create Eve out of Adam's
side a form of parity between man and woman seems evident: 'bone'
of his 'bone', 'flesh' of his 'flesh' (2.23), or even complementarity, as
Trible argues (1978: 94–105). Although woman clearly images man,
she is neither identical nor equal, despite the exegetical attempts
of feminist theologians (Clines 1990: 25–48). This imaging has to
be interrogated beyond the superficial notion of apparent parity – a
type of mirror image. Although she is recognised as the same species
as Adam, as opposed to the other creatures he was presented with,
she is different. And it is because she is different from Adam that
she is his subordinate: created specifically for his need, and

created to help him fulfil the commandment, 'Be fruitful and multiply' (Gen. 1.28). As Adam is ontologically unable to be God's equal, so Eve cannot be Adam's equal.

This first couple provide the blueprint for normative citizenship in the theocracy proposed in the Bible's first story. Mimesis is the key to its organisation and power relations. The one act that signals a departure from this structure, the taking of the fruit from the tree of knowledge of good and evil, is presented in the biblical narrative as a catalyst for an intensification of power relations. The man's relationship with the earth becomes focused on its subjugation, and it is recognised as a relationship of struggle. Likewise, the relationship between the man and the woman becomes focused on her subjectivity. The man is the focus of her desire, and the effect on her is now made explicit: he rules over her. The serpent's promise achieves a limited fulfilment – the man is more evidently God through his exercise of physical labour in the visualisation of subduing the earth and in his role as master of the woman. But to be like God is not to be God – mimesis, as can be demonstrated from Plato to contemporary identity theory, is a power tool. To imitate means never to perfectly replicate and, thereby, imitation consistently reinforces and reaffirms the object of imitation. Although humanity is liberated from the nursery of Eden, it remains in the memory and the constancy of the divine will at work within subsequent biblical literature ensures that any liberation is relative.

The basic pattern of psychological accounts of identity formation do resonate with the story of the first couple: the realisation of the self as subject is attained through a process of initial identification with an 'other', followed by the distinction of the self from that 'other' based on the realisation of difference. Identifying imitation, or the *imago dei*, as the key to understanding the biblical account of human identity in relation to God, does tempt a quasi-Freudian Oedipus/Electra reading of Genesis (see Rashkow 2000: 43–73). Indeed, Jules Lacan's development of Freudian symbols through recourse to linguistic theory is particularly compelling (Piskorowski 1992; Parker 1999). In a Lacanian reading of the Adam and Eve story God can assume dual roles of mother and father: as mother creating and nurturing the first couple, and as father, 'his prohibitions are given, and his authoritative voice is heard' (Piskorowski 1992: 314). Or, as the authors of *The Postmodern Bible* express it, 'God's word imparts structure to the formless female earth' (Aichele *et al.* 1995: 213). Kim Parker's Lacanian reading of the story, however, observes the role of the mother in the appearance of Eve, in that she is the mirror reflection to which Adam exclaims, 'Bones of my bone, flesh of my flesh!', just as Lacan's mother-figure mirrors, or signifies, an identification that can never be truly realised by the child, or the signified (Lacan 1977). As soon as Adam names his 'mirror' he distinguishes himself from it:

> So, although his language tries to express his desire for unity (אִישׁ and אִשָּׁה) his language only articulates the distinction between the self and the Other (that is, the woman is not אִישׁ but אִשָּׁה).
>
> (Parker 1999: 26)

To move out of the mirror stage to full maturity Adam and Eve both need to be confronted by, in Lacan's terminology, the 'law of the Name-of-the-Father' or the 'phallus'. For Lacan, the phallus, or rather the lack of the phallus, is the key to the maturation process that is characterised by a sense of loss; also, the phallus is not a penis, but a symbol of unattainable power – unattainable to both men and women. Parker identifies the tree of knowledge as the phallus in the Genesis story:

> The result of the eating of the fruit is, interestingly enough, not plenitude, or a fulfilment of desire, or even a knowledge of good and evil, but a 'knowledge of nakedness', that is, of sexual differentiation, or knowledge of a Lacanian 'lack'.
>
> (Parker 1999: 28)

Hence human existence is in essence a constant process of longing for the impossible and grieving for its loss, but humans have attained maturity as social beings. This psychoanalytical reading of Adam and Eve's story both supports an understanding of the first couple as children in personality, if not physical, terms, and accounts for the tension of the story that describes a maturation process that is distressing yet liberating. Of course, it is not impossible that the biblical writers could have anticipated Freud or even Lacan, since these theories at their most basic level simply try to account for the way things are in terms of being human. This is precisely what the writers of the story tried to do in their observations of recurring power relations played out in a theocratic context. As Shulamith Firestone comments, Freud is more useful for describing power relations than for providing a credible explanation of them: 'his genius was poetic rather than scientific; his ideas are more valuable as metaphors than as literal truths' (1979: 50). Man in his exercise of power is, to all intents and purposes, God in the world, but in the imitation of godlike, absolute power he falls short. Subversion of these versions of reality might be achieved by dispensing with the father-God, and then the man is free to exercise absolute power. Woman, by experiencing subjectivity in the face of male power, can imagine and even aspire to autonomy. Judith Butler neatly sums up this two-edged process: 'The analysis of subjection is always double, tracing the conditions of subject formation and tracing the turn against those conditions for the subject – and its perspective – to emerge' (1997: 29). Subversive deconstruction of the normative boundaries is evident from the very beginning of the Bible: God commands, but he is disobeyed. It is the woman who actively disobeys, and that is a clear signal to the reader encountering the rest of the Bible. We must watch out for the women, but, from the story of Eve onwards, the enigma lies in not knowing whose side she is on.

To argue that the biblical account of creation and human 'becoming' presents a patriarchal sexual hierarchy is an argument that has been well rehearsed down the centuries. Despite feminist theologians' attempts to 'depatriarchalise' this narrative, it remains the foundation text for essentialist gender construction in traditional religions. A closer examination of the mimetic model employed in this biblical narrative reveals that the construction of power relations limits male as well as female parameters. Both male and female characters remain in a relationship of infantile dependency – whether as good or bad offspring.

Through her critique of the notion of 'woman', Luce Irigaray offers the concept of mimesis as a means of evolving identity that emanates actively rather than passively from the self (1985). Her use of mimesis both recognises its potential in terms of the model's power, and explores how the imitator parodies the model in its inevitable state of incompletion. Thus Irigaray uses the concept of mimesis – so popular with psychoanalysts in explaining human identity crises and often as an affirmation of female subjectivity – as a means of enabling reconstructed ways of being 'woman'. Butler neatly sums up Irigaray's 'repetition and displacement of the phallic economy' when discussing her deconstruction of materiality in Plato's *Timaeus*:

the reinscription of the maternal takes place by writing with and through the language of phallic philosophemes. This textual practice is not grounded in a rival ontology, but inhabits – indeed, penetrates, occupies, and redeploys – the paternal language itself.

(1993: 45)

In classical thought phallocentric constructions inevitably and relentlessly reinforce the ascendancy of the first sex; in biblical thought human maleness constantly and consistently defers to the deity. Though, obviously, to a less intensive extent than that of 'becoming female', this theological dimension to male consciousness does expose the problematic of 'becoming male'. The foundation myth presents a maleness in divine form constructed beyond the human realm and, although that myth is obviously the product of male experience, it reflects a notion of powerlessness that was only fully confronted and dealt with in relatively modern times with the Enlightenment myth of the 'rise of man'. Inevitably, in our era, the biblical notion of power in relation to 'man' has been read through Enlightenment eyes – both by men and by feminist scholars who have translated their experience of patriarchy into the ancient world (Daly 1973), and have not taken into account that male power is relative and not absolute. In the world constructed by the biblical writers – a world that intensively informed western and colonial patterns of existence from the fourth century to the dawn of modernity – Irigaray's notion of mimesis might offer a way forward for both male and female identities to be re-formed, once freed from the psychological state of self-subjection as divine offspring.

The stories in Genesis inevitably reflect ancient Near Eastern feudalism in its varying degrees of aspiring to absolute power. God as the ultimate king exercises supreme control over his kingdom – in this case the whole of creation. In such a scheme the king's subjects are in a position of total subjugation, their quality of life largely dependent on the character and ability of their monarch. This feudal-type dependency is most immediately encapsulated by the image of paternalism, and throughout the biblical canons, both Jewish and Christian versions, the image of God as father emerges to reinforce the nature of divine/human relations:

> Is he not your father, who
> created you,
> who made you and
> established you?

(Deut. 32.6; see Chapter 1, this volume)

And:

> Has the rain a father,
> or who has begotten the drops
> of dew? From whose womb did the ice
> come forth,
> and who has given birth to the
> hoarfrost of heaven?

(Job 38.28–9)

This passage from the book of Job occurs in the course of the most powerful divine diatribe in the Bible. Job has dared to question the integrity of God, and the reply is a mighty reiteration of divine omnipotence and omniscience with the image of parent at its core. In this most forceful of statements both male and female images of procreation are utilised, ensuring that God is the unique parent – the creator of the universe. Despite the image of this God giving birth, the text is not presenting us with a female deity, since God remains a male subject throughout biblical discourse. Although the language of paternalism for God is recurrent in the Jewish and Christian canons, it would be simplistic to assume that the ideas conveyed are static. As social, political and cultural experiences develop and change, so does the concept of God as father. God creates and 'fathers' Adam and Eve in a way that is symptomatic of his role throughout biblical literature. He is the absolute, un-attainable power, indistinguishable from the tree of knowledge, or phallus, in the midst of the Garden, since he created it. Adam and Eve never really move on from their 'mirror' stage. Their longing draws them back, and God calls them, and their descendants, back to the garden.

The early chapters of Genesis inevitably express the status quo by suggesting mythic explanations for *why* things might be the way they are. This might seem an over-obvious point, but by making it we can more easily divulge the purpose of these myths and their effect in the biblical scheme. By beginning with these myths and stories the reader becomes drawn into the biblical world and begins to share in its values, its hopes and its fears. When later texts present their readers with the laws that govern this world, these laws make sense, since they reflect familiar situations, upholding and challenging the behaviour patterns of individuals within a known societal framework (Carmichael 1974). When we eventually encounter the Ten Commandments in Exodus, we are already familiar with the God that we are commanded to love exclusively. Through our encounter with the text we know the terrible reper- cussions for murder, and we have experienced the problems of jealousy with siblings and with partners, the damage caused by adul- tery and stealing, and so on. The boundaries have been set. God is in place, omnipotent and omniscient, and humanity – men, women, children, kinsmen, strangers, slaves – and all living creatures know their place.

LAW

In the opening chapters of Genesis the triangular relationship of God/man/woman is set in place to explain and inform subsequent narrative and legislation as it unfolds. The reader has the necessary framework to read the codes and recognise proper and improper behaviour. Thus, the texts that follow from the foundation account often confirm and extend the set sexual/familial/social/political boundaries – a tendency well illustrated from the Wisdom litera- ture, and we will look at some examples from this genre later on. It is this confirmation of the given boundaries that concerns us in this chapter, but we need to bear in mind that this process of demar- cation can be read as the necessary counterpart or antithesis to the Bible's central thesis – the *un*bounded power of God.

Both Leviticus and Deuteronomy list practices that are תועבות (Deut. 14.3, 17.1; Lev. 18.26–30), a term traditionally translated as 'abominations'; also, the practitioner is 'abhorrent' (תועבת) to the deity (Deut. 22.5). Contemporary scholarship rejects the idea that תועבה conveys such a moralistic overtone, and removes it to a more neutral socio-religious frame to mean the 'transgression of borders' (Boyarin 1995: 334, n. 3). While noting that תועבה may not mean the same in each context in which it appears in the biblical text, Olyan comments, 'Usage in general suggests the violation of a socially constructed boundary, the undermining or reversal of what is conventional, the order of things as the ancient might see it' (1994: 180, n. 3). These practices are extremely wide-ranging, and include dealings with unclean animals (Deut. 14.3), defective sacri- fices (Deut. 17.1), cross-dressing (Deut. 22.5) and certain sexual acts (Lev. 18.22); and in Proverbs the word can refer to those who are responsible for the miscarriage of justice. תועבה is a term that signi- fies the deeper levels of the boundaries drawn at creation that denote God's world – who/what is 'in' and who/what is 'out'.

One passage from the legislative literature of the Bible that highlights the importance of maintaining order in sexual relations is found in the section of Leviticus known as the 'forbidden degrees'. These are listed in chapter 18, and in chapter 20 the penalties are listed for those who practise them. The term תועבה occurs in 18.26 to sum up the nature of the practices that have been described in the previous verses, as well as in the particular proscription against intercourse between men in 18.22. As usual in biblical legislative literature the text presumes a male readership (Brenner 1994: 255–8), and its concern lies primarily with preserving the integrity of the men of the community and their family boundaries.

The 'forbidden degrees' list inappropriate sexual partners for Israelite men and, like the biblical food laws, this text has attracted myriad theories as to its origin and meaning from anthropologists, sociologists and psychoanalysts, as well as from theologians and biblical scholars. This list does not simply comprise prohibitions against incestuous practices, since a number of the forbidden relations do not involve common blood. To be more precise, many of the 'forbidden degrees' are concerned with the preservation of family boundaries or, more explicitly, the boundaries of any one patriarch's realm. Any sexual coupling that blurs these boundaries is forbidden. This includes, for example, relations between stepbrothers and stepsisters, whether or not they share a blood link, and relations with aunts and daughters-in-law. These individuals are part of one patriarch's family, and this primary identity would become confused if they became associated with a male who has formed, or will form, his own family group.

Among the 'forbidden degrees' we find the infamous verse that has been used down the centuries in western and colonial worlds to legislate against, and ostracise from society, those who practise homosexual acts: 'You shall not lie with a male as with a woman; it is an abomination' (Lev. 18.22). In recent times the interpretation of this verse as a prohibition against homosexual relations in general has been challenged by commentators (Olyan 1994; Boyarin 1995). In liberal Jewish and Christian confessional contexts a common way to deal with the prohibition has been to relativise it as a reaction against ancient non-Israelite cultic settings, an explanation that traditional biblical scholarship has offered in the past. Thus, the prohibition is seen to belong to a cultic rather than a social context and to be meaningless in our own contemporary world.

Without wanting to argue that such a prohibitive attitude to homosexual acts should have any relevance today, we can suggest that it is not a convincing strategy to draw clear lines between cultic practices, alien or familiar, and social values and experience. The two contexts are intertwined, existing in a relationship that can be mutually dependent and affirmative but also reactive and dis-consonant. The cultic characteristics mirror the social order, while the cult can expose a society's vulnerability. Whether the Egyptians and Canaanites practised cultic homosexual acts is a central question to be addressed in any study of those ancient societies and their religious beliefs and practices. In terms of exploring biblical meaning, however, the focus should rest on the transposition of this phenomenon, whether consciously or not, into one of a list of prohibitions that are not universally cultic. The restrictions on familial relations can be read as clear boundaries set up to preserve patriarchal 'territories'. The restriction on homosexual intercourse, and the restriction on bestiality that immediately follows in the text (Lev. 18.23), can also be read as boundary markers. One demarcates maleness and the other humanness. It follows then that, in the case of bestiality, the prohibition applies to both men and women.

These distinctions take us back to the opening chapters of Genesis, but here the legislation spells out more clearly the primary distinctions between male/female and human/animal. When the animals were paraded in front of Adam he recognised no 'partner'. Adam's need for a partner, a 'helper' (Gen. 2.18), has always been a magnet for commentators from Augustine to contemporary feminist scholars. Augustine argued that it is clear from the biblical text that this need for help lay entirely within the sphere of reproduction (*Literal Meaning of Genesis* IX: 5) – an argument upheld, reluctantly, in recent scholarship by David Clines (1990: 36). This counters Phyllis Trible's interpretation of Adam and Eve as being created within a relationship of perfect complementarity (see page 23). The centrality of reproduction as the key to Eve's role is an even more convincing explanation if we look at Genesis 2 in the light of Leviticus 18.

Sexual acts between two men as they are expressed in biblical texts compromise male power because the male who is penetrated is emasculated – he is likened to a woman. Likewise, inappropriate touching of male genitalia by a woman, although expedient, attracts extreme retribution that can be understood in the context of avoiding confusion regarding gender identity (Carmichael 1974: 234; Landy 1997: 170):

> If men get into a fight with one another, and the wife of
> one intervenes to rescue her husband from the grip of his

opponent by reaching out and seizing his genitals, you shall cut off her hand; show no pity.

(Deut. 25.11–12)

The woman might seem to be taking the initiative in sexual matters and, in doing so, takes on a male role.

Deuteronomy also contains another prohibition against behaviour that more explicitly confuses gender identity: 'A woman shall not wear a man's apparel, nor shall a man put on a woman's garment; for whoever does such things is abhorrent to the Lord your God' (22.5). This verse, like the Leviticus verses prohibiting homosexual practices and bestiality, has been interpreted as a reactionary response to foreign cultic practice – in this case, the ancient Mesopotamian cult of Ishtar. The picture of the lascivious world of cultic prostitution, painted with particular confidence by biblical scholars, is heavily underpinned by one source, Herodotus' *Historiae*, to form a stark contrast between God's holy nation and its pagan neighbours. This use of the evidence has been viewed with increasing suspicion by contemporary classical scholars (Beard and Henderson 1998). The backcloth of rampant, universally practised, cultic prostitution, against which biblical moral imperatives were set, is a decreasingly credible scenario:

> Each set of cultural historians has fed on the other's conviction that the lack, dubiety and paucity of corroborating evidence to set beside Herodotus' is a happenstance that can be effaced by a mixture of extrapolation with imagination.
>
> (Beard and Henderson 1998: 65)

Cultic prostitution is dealt with as a separate issue in other biblical texts, where the emphasis is placed on the 'wages of sin', rather than the actual sexual practices (Deut. 23.18; see also 1 Kings 14.24). Cultic prostitution, for males and females, was obviously practised in the ancient Near East, and it is equally clear that the biblical writers wanted to draw a clear contrast between such practices and the ideal behaviour set out for God's holy nation. What is evident also is that cultic prostitution is not the only context of male homosexual practice that is recognised and forbidden by these writers.

Olyan's extensive study of Leviticus 18.22 and 20.13 (1994: 179–206) demonstrates that the prohibition in these verses is primarily concerned with anal intercourse between males. Rather than being a reaction against foreign cults, Olyan, following Bigger

(1979), Eilberg-Schwartz (1990) and others, demonstrates that purity laws provide a key to the prohibitions in general in Leviticus 18 and 20. Taking this insight further, Olyan, again following Bigger, focuses on the concept of 'mixing', but, unlike other commentators, applies it specifically to the prohibition against male coupling. Olyan concludes that the author of the Holiness Code (Leviticus 17–26), who was responsible for the prohibition, included it because this sexual act can involve the mixing of two defiling emissions – semen and excrement. However, he suggests the original reason for generating the prohibition might lie in the transgressing of boundaries:

> Perhaps the insertive partner was originally condemned as a boundary violator because his act 'feminized' his partner or because he did not conform to his class (male) when he chose another male as a partner in intercourse.
>
> (1994: 206)

Boyarin parallels Foucault's analysis of sexuality in relation to ancient classical society (1988) with an analysis of biblical and talmudic culture. He concludes that:

> The element common to both classical culture (with all of its variations) and biblical culture (with all of its variations), is that the taboos and tolerances of the cultural vis-à-vis same-sex genital practice were tied precisely to structures of maleness and femaleness, to gender and not to a putative sexuality.
>
> (1995: 354)

There is no concept of naming an individual as 'homosexual' or 'heterosexual' or of defining them in terms of their sexuality. It is the particular practice of anal intercourse between males that causes the problem and attracts the prohibition – because it is a practice that confuses gender and, by extension, power relations.

Such interpretations as those of Olyan and Boyarin are certainly more credible than attempts at cultic explanations, or exegesis that reads back into ancient texts modern definitions of sexuality. The interpretations offered by Olyan and Boyarin for Leviticus 18.22 are more convincing when we take the context of the verse seriously. Leviticus 18–20 is intrinsically concerned with social and family matters rather than specifically cultic ones. Where religion is concerned the stress is on the supremacy of Israel's God over other 'false' deities, or forbidding practices that are distinct from the socio-religious culture of God's holy people, including the use of idols, tattoos, and wizards. These chapters epitomise the problems engendered in separating out social concerns from religious ones – certainly in the context of ancient Israel, and probably in most ancient Near Eastern societies. Recent research on ancient Corinth reveals the paucity of evidence for cultic practices. This weakens any argument that would base the city's hedonistic reputation on pagan rituals. Indeed, a more convincing argument is that liberal social sexual practices were simply mirrored by the religious: '*all* its women were, truly, goddesses of love' (Beard and Henderson 1998: 73).

In biblical terms, homosexual acts are judged primarily to be infringements of familial/social boundaries rather than acts that are associated with 'foreign' cults. This conclusion is supported by the narrative accounts of Lot and his daughters in Genesis 19 and the Levite and his concubine in Judges 19. In these stories the most extreme antisocial behaviour is manifested in attempted homosexual gang rape, and this behaviour is set in sharp contrast to the obligation to offer hospitality to those who are alien to your homeland – it is the antithesis, indeed, of the injunction to 'love the alien as yourself' in Leviticus 19.34. In both stories, in Genesis and in Judges, there is the good host; in both stories there are violent local men; and in both stories women are proffered as a means of diverting the worst atrocity imaginable – the rape of men by men (see Chapter 4, this volume).

The divine decrees laid down for sexual behaviour reveal a key concern with maintaining clear boundaries between male and female roles. It is not surprising in this patriarchal context to find that male interests are central, and that the boundaries set for sexual encounters reflect an attitude of possession towards female family members. In biblical legislation and narrative sexual relations outside marriage are restricted in order to protect the property of fathers and husbands. This can be illustrated by the placing of teaching on appropriate behaviour towards other men's daughters and on adultery (Deut. 22.13–30) beside a variety of prescriptions that are mainly to do with lost property and appropriate neighbourly behaviour (22.1–12). The stories of Lot's daughters and the unnamed concubine clearly show that the protection of property has to take second place to the protection of 'maleness'. It is preferable to cross a property boundary than a gender boundary. The former might compromise power through the perceived loss of wealth in the broadest sense, but the latter compromises power structures through the confusion of the order of creation itself.

The classified list of sleeping partners in Leviticus 18 reinforces the boundaries that are set up in Genesis 1–3. The commands in the former, uttered by the male God to his male audience, mediated by Moses, authenticate the primary relationship grounded in creation between God and Adam. In the theocracy described in the book of Leviticus man remains in intimate imitation of God, and this status has to be protected from contamination and confusion. Familial relations have to have clear lines of demarcation to protect patrilinear descent and the male power base itself.

If we move forwards through the biblical narrative from the setting of primary boundaries that demarcate between what is divine, male, female and animal, we discover a second set of boundaries. These are placed around particular sections of humanity through the concept of election, which unfolds in the story of God's choice of Abraham and Sarah as the parents of the chosen nation. This boundary is reinforced through legislation that ensures that Israel, the custodians of the Torah, can be a holy nation (Lev. 17–26). The notion of 'holiness' ensures that this exclusivity is carved out even further *among* God's elect, where Israelite men and women are included or excluded by virtue of their behaviour. God's absolute power extends into every corner of their lives, not only in terms of how they should worship, but also in terms of how they look after their animals, how they do business, how they eat, how they have sex, how they treat strangers, how they control their children, and so on. This intrusive character of Israelite religion – this all-inclusive cradle-to-grave package – was distinctive in the ancient Near East, and was a characteristic that would be inherited by Judaism and Christianity in the Graeco-Roman world. Where other nations distinguished between the roles of gods and governments, Israel fused them – at least according to the biblical evidence. Nothing lay outside divine jurisdiction, from an individual's inner feelings about another's possessions – 'You shall not covet your neighbour's house' (Exod. 20.17) – to the appointment of the nation's rulers, whether they be patriarchs, judges or kings. In the world of the biblical writers there are no boundaries to divine jurisdiction, only boundaries that the divine imposes on the created world.

WISDOM

> When the Lord created his works from the beginning, and, in making them, determined their boundaries, he arranged his works in an eternal order and their domination for all generations.
>
> (Sir. 16.26–7; see also Ps. 104)

The authors of the biblical wisdom tradition take a conservative line in explaining that the boundaries set up by divine decree are advantageous to human existence. Without such boundaries there would be chaos – in fact the world itself would cease to exist. This anarchic picture is realised in the apocalyptic imagination of prophets who dared to conceive of a world at the mercy of divine a-creative power: 'I looked to the earth, and lo, it was waste and void (תהו ובהו)' (Jer. 4.23; contrast Gen. 1.2).

In the didactic literature the creator God reappears and reminds us that setting up the universe was only the beginning of his work. The same power that brought the world into being constantly sustains it in every conceivable dimension and, thus, from the human perspective it is vital to grasp the knowledge that 'the fear of God is the beginning of wisdom' (Prov. 9.10). Realising the pivotal role of the divine in existence allows humanity to understand its relative position, and that of the rest of creation, and this recognition of created order works to reinforce it. The didactic literature of the Hebrew Bible takes the notion of creation beyond its materiality to the metaphysical realm, where the concept of wisdom is explained in terms of an immanent divine presence in the world. Wisdom allows God to exist outside the transcendent heavenly realm, and to permeate every corner of life on the earth. Wisdom is present to ensure the seasons come and go, to imbue governments with wise counsel and judges with discernment, and to help men choose good wives and parents to instruct their children.

This systematic understanding of world order is reminiscent of stoicism, popular in the hellenistic world from the late fourth century BCE, where logic, physics and ethics – inextricably bound together – comprise the holistic understanding of existence. In this sense the notion of wisdom evident in Israelite religion can be said to represent its philosophical dimension, although it does fundamentally differ from Greek philosophical systems in its essentially religious outlook. Such a meeting of the religious and the philosophical is not explicit in the context of Greek thought, and it is not until the period of the Roman Empire and the renaissance of earlier schools through Neoplatonism and other gnostic systems that a theistic element is clearly discernible. In the biblical tradition the apparent mutually exclusive notions of a self-sustaining universe – whether the result of providential physical laws or the presence of universal wisdom – and an interventionist deity come together in a paradoxical account of reality. The biblical wisdom-writers anticipate, or parallel, the explanations of the universe and the uniqueness of human experience offered by the Greek philosophical schools. The ideas about wisdom in the Israelite tradition can be applied to supersede Greek philosophical speculation through the addition of an omniscient deity that is responsible for the sustaining element of the universe and has the potential power to subvert it at will. This synthesis of philosophy with monotheistic religion is characteristic of Philo of Alexandria's work, which presented the God of early Judaism in similar terms in relation to the popular versions of first century CE schools of thought.

While the wisdom literature contains references to wisdom as the sustaining element in creation and presents ideas that can be set beside philosophies that emanate from the élite intelligentsia of hellenistic societies, it also contains instruction or observations that can simply be termed 'common sense' (Camp 1985; following Geertz 1973). In Israelite literature, in common with its ancient Near Eastern parallels, the concept of wisdom embraces both abstract and mundane observations – wisdom is the hidden ingredient that sustains both the world and our everyday experiences of life. What is of particular interest for this study is that this natural order is not a pre-existent integral factor of the created world, such as providence or fate, as the philosophers might argue, and neither is it a created aspect implanted into the world by the deity. Instead, it is a phenomenon that is constantly and actively controlled by the deity. In her study of Proverbs, Camp argues:

> For the ancient Yahwists, the religious lens through which Israel's common sense, whether that of clan or court, always looked included the view of Yahweh (and Yahweh alone) as determiner.
>
> (1985: 162)

She refers to Prov. 26.27 to illustrate this point: 'Whoever digs a pit will fall into it, and a stone will come back on the one who starts it rolling.' And she comments:

There is no warrant for imagining some other force at work here besides Yahweh, who (needless to say, 'of course') created the digger, the stone, and the roller and set them in relationship to each other.

(1985: 163)

This understanding of the 'experiential wisdom' in Proverbs is in stark contrast to that of traditional biblical scholars (particularly, McKane 1970 and von Rad 1972a). These scholars have argued that a dichotomy exists within the wisdom tradition between 'experiential wisdom' and 'Yahwistic wisdom', the former stemming from the educated élite – the civil service centred on the court and dating from the time of Solomon – and the latter, usually understood to represent a later strand, from the religious, perhaps more 'lowly', sectors of society. These positions that present such clear divisions between the religious and the secular are untenable in the light of recent anthropological and cultural studies and, in contrast, present an unconvincing picture of how ancient societies operated. Such a dichotomy between the religious and the secular reflects a particular view of modernity rather than antiquity. The world-view that dominates biblical texts never loses sight of the omnipresent omnipotent divine, whose pivotal position is never compromised.

The all-embracing totality of divine rule is nowhere more clearly expressed than in a scene from another piece of wisdom literature: the theophany described in Job 38–41. In this passage God bombards Job with a series of rhetorical questions that make him confront the magnitude of divine creation and the God that sustains both the physical and the metaphysical realities. This is presented as the ultimate response to Job's own naive questioning of the Almighty:

Where were you when I laid the
foundation of the earth? . . .

Have you commanded the
morning since your days began
and caused the dawn to know
its place . . .?

Do you give the horse its might?
Do you clothe its neck with
mane?

Is it by your wisdom that the
hawk soars,
and spreads its wings toward
the south?

Is it at your command that the
eagle mounts up
and makes its nest on high?

(38.4, 12; 39.19, 26–7)

This revelation prompts the appropriate human response from Job:
'I know that you can do all things, and that no purpose of yours can
be thwarted' (42.2). And regretting having dared to question the
ways of God, in the light of this divine confrontation Job concludes,
'Therefore I despise myself, and repent in dust and ashes' (42.6).
This scene neatly encapsulates the biblical concept of divine/human
hierarchy (see Chapter 7 below). There is no pantheon of gods to
relativise divine attributes or domain. God is all and in all:

For thus says the Lord,
who created the heavens
(he is God!),
who formed the earth and
made it
(he established it;
he did not create it in chaos,
he formed it to be inhabited!):
I am the Lord, and there is
no other.

(Isa. 45.18)

In subsequent Christian theology the same omniscience and
omnipresence is expressed by the glorified Son of God: 'I am the
Alpha and the Omega, the first and the last, the beginning and the
end' (Rev. 22.13). But the son's subjection to the father-God ensures
that, at least in Christian biblical tradition, such power is simply
an extension of that of the parent. Early Christian theologies of
power will be discussed in more detail in Chapter 6.

As in the case of biblical legislation, wisdom teaching is a male
affair – presented primarily as the male God advising men –
although women are included at times, for example in the context

of advice on parenting. Paradoxically, a notion of the female does figure in a most prominent way in this literature with 'wisdom' itself, a feminine noun in Hebrew (חוכמה), personified as a woman.

> Get wisdom; get insight: do not forget or turn away from the words of my mouth. Do not forsake her, and she will keep you; love her, and she will guard you.
>
> (Prov. 4.5–6)

The use of a female figure to personify wisdom has been heralded as a sign of hope by reformist feminist biblical scholars and theologians, who utilise it to unearth and develop the concept of the feminine face of the divine in a tradition where imagery is predominantly male. Ancient Near Eastern goddess cults have been explored in the search to find clues to the origins of Lady Wisdom. This search has not yielded conclusive evidence, but it does offer a range of possibilities that include feminine deities from a number of places – Egypt, Mesopotamia and Canaan itself. While these goddesses suggest parallels to the symbolism that accompanies the presentation of Lady Wisdom, there are none that coincide with the breadth of meaning expressed through personified wisdom.

Early twentieth-century scholarship produced theories supported by ancient Near Eastern material that were not wholly convincing. Albright's research suggested a line of tradition for Lady Wisdom that traced her from Semitic sources over three millennia (1920). With such a vast timescale any attempted reconstruction in terms of continuity of meaning inevitably loses credibility. A contemporary parallel would be to see the veneration of the Virgin Mary in contemporary English Catholicism in direct descent from a tenth-century BCE, southern European local religion – not impossible, but also not overtly helpful in attempting to understand Mary's significance in early twenty-first-century theology and practice.

The goddess Asherah, who was a well-attested figure in the Canaanite pantheon (known as Athirat or Elat, the consort of El in Ugaritic texts), offers a more vivid and convincing backcloth against which to set Lady Wisdom, particularly in terms of chronology and geography. A recent synthesis contained in Judith McKinlay's exposition of the wisdom concept offers a viable pathway through the maze of current theories on this subject (1996: 17–37). There is archaeological evidence to link Asherah with Yahweh (from Kuntillet 'Ajrud and Khirbet el-Qôm), and there are biblical texts that refer to 'Asherah', for example the Asherah made by King

Jeroboam (1 Kings 14.15). Many diverse interpretations have arisen, prompted by the complex concept of Asherah – whether the term refers to a goddess or a type of religious structure (Margalit 1990; Olyan 1988).

In sum, the evidence suggests a less monotheistic early heritage for Israelite religion than that preferred by the biblical writers who were responsible for the extant shape and form of biblical literature. If popular religion within Israel at one time did include the notion of a female consort for Yahweh, or simply recognised a feminine aspect within the religious framework of the cult, then the appearance of Lady Wisdom would be consonant in terms of the religious psychology of the intended audiences for biblical texts such as the Proverbs. Although the texts might tap into this folk memory, the way in which she is then presented in these texts ensures that Lady Wisdom is neither equal to nor independent from the all-powerful Yahweh.

Through the images used to portray her and in the words that have been put into her mouth by the biblical writers, Lady Wisdom subsumes symbols and ideas from diverse times and places in the ancient Near East, though most particularly from Canaan itself. But she is more than this – she is both a composite and a parody of those ancient goddesses. The biblical writers have taken familiar images and themes from known popular goddess religion and transformed them into one aspect of a religion that is focused on a male deity, Yahweh, the deity who, from the biblical writers' stance, is the one true god who creates and sustains the universe. Lady Wisdom is not a goddess, a singular deity, but another manifestation of the biblical God's divine will. This development could be understood as an appropriation of the goddess by the biblical writers who ensure that her attractions are subsumed into their particular theistic framework. In a speech given to Lady Wisdom she places herself firmly in a subordinate role to the Lord Yahweh: 'The Lord created me at the beginning of his work, the first of his acts of long ago' (יהוה קנני ראשית דרכו קדם מפעליו מאז) (Prov. 8.22). In order to accentuate the attributes of Lady Wisdom, the writers of Proverbs develop a poetic parallelism and introduce a 'femina negativa' – the foreign woman, or 'outsider' (אשה זרה). Though standing in stark contrast to one another, these are two female figures with a common prey: human males. Men are presented as gullible creatures who can follow the attractions of either figure, unaware that one offers merely transitory pleasure that will ultimately lead to ruin, whereas the other leads to prosperity and life:

Say to wisdom, 'You are my
sister',
and call insight your intimate
friend,
that they may keep you away from the
loose woman (אשה זרה),
from the adulteress (נכריה) with her
smooth words.

(Prov. 7.4)

The NRSV translation moves the meaning of אשה זרה from the more
literal 'non-Israelite' woman, to a moralistic frame of reference. This
is justified through the pairing of זרה with נכריה when this figure
is described in Proverbs. Camp identifies a clear link between the
negation of this figure and post-exilic teaching against foreign
women prompted by the threat of polluting the nation through
marriage with such women (1985: 268–71). Although not negating
them, this backdrop for the foreign woman does take the emphasis
away from theories that see in this 'femina negativa' the shadow of
an ancient Near Eastern goddess, evoked by the writers of Proverbs
in order to be shown up conclusively as inferior to the Lordship of
Yahweh – a god who subsumes a greater concept of the feminine
divine within himself.

Whether the dark shadow of an ancient goddess does lurk behind
the figure of Lady Wisdom found in the biblical didactic tradition,
or whether she can be discerned within the composite figure of
Lady Wisdom's foreign antithesis, are not questions that can be
given objective answers. The evidence does suggest that goddess
worship was common practice in ancient Canaan prior to and con-
current with the emergence of Yahwism. The evidence from the
biblical wisdom literature uniformly presents us with a theological framework that convincingly subsumes this potential divine
rival as a created attribute of Yahweh, or demonises her by transforming her into a female figure that destroys men both morally and
materially.

To subvert this framework, Claudia Camp encourages readers of
Proverbs to read the 'foreign', or 'strange', woman against the grain
of the text, 'with its power to pit one woman against another' (1997;
and 2000, where this approach is extended to other texts concerning 'strangeness'). She invites fellow readers to identify with this
personification of the 'other':

42

We read, rather, to use an image from folklore, as tricksters, those two-sided characters who appear both as creators and disruptors of social order, whose flaunting of the boundaries of social convention is embraced as part of the life-giving fabric, whose strangeness is acknowledged as part and parcel of their wisdom. We read as Strange Women.

(1997: 108)

The created order set into the universe is poetically personified in female form and, in parallel, the anarchic antithesis to divine order is also represented as a woman, and both figures call men to them. The most 'unreal' of these figures is Wisdom who, though created by God, is pre-existent with God as he creates the world, and can make such claims as, 'By me kings reign and rulers decree what is just' (Prov. 8.15). The אשה זרה is more easily identified as a 'loose woman', who lacks moral integrity and whose seductive words and actions are not alien to human experience:

Come, let us take our fill of love
until morning;
let us delight ourselves with
love.
For my husband is not at home . . .

With much seductive speech she
persuades him;
with her smooth talk she
compels him.
Right away he follows her,
and goes like an ox to the
slaughter . . .
He is like a bird rushing into a
snare,
not knowing that it will cost
him his life.

(Prov. 7.18–23)

With Lady Wisdom humanity is portrayed in a negative light, with a form of womanhood placed far beyond any experience that human womanhood could identify with, and men presented as gullible prey who are incapable of making any autonomous moral choice. The boundaries of morality and order are the product of divine will and,

43

following the pattern of Adam and Eve, human beings are placed in the position of respondents to given options, rather than the initiators or agents of moral choice. We will see in the next chapter, in the story of Tamar, how the biblical writers can use the breaking of these boundaries, can even vindicate the אשה זרה, to express their God's omnipotence.

The three categories utilised in this chapter to investigate the setting of boundaries in the biblical world-view – creation, law and wisdom – encompass the totality of human experience materially and metaphysically. The biblical God is all and in all – transcendent and immanent. The next chapter explores how these boundaries inscribed for human existence provide the stage for 'God to be God' – to be everything and anything other than human – through transgressing, indeed exploding, these limits fixed for mortals.

3

TESTING THE
BOUNDARIES

PICKING UP THE PIECES

In Chapter 1 we identified a category of texts that appear to challenge patriarchy and infer its reform, if not its end. These texts can be read almost as parodies of traditional polarisation of masculine and feminine prescribed behaviour. Genesis, in particular, has been a rich resource for feminist biblical scholars who have worked to uncover positive accounts of active female characters. In this text we encounter the matriarchs of the biblical tradition – Sarah, Rebecca and Rachel – and in Genesis 28 we have the ultimate exposé of patriarchal culture executed by the deeply-wronged Tamar. Genesis will be the focus of this chapter where we will look in particular at the theme of challenging the gender boundaries we identified in the previous chapter. In Chapter 4 we will discuss how this theme intensifies in Judges and Ruth, and in Chapter 5 we will extend this critique to biblical texts that reflect contexts within the Hellenistic and Roman empires.

The book of Genesis is the product of many cultural contexts in its long history of textual evolution – ancient Near Eastern agrarian society, tribal cultures and feudal style city states, not to mention the influence of much later Persian times (van Seters 1992; Albertz 1994; Lemche 1993) – and, as such, it escapes mercurially from attempts at any singular, particular enculturalisation. Scholars of modernity submitted Genesis and its pentateuchal bedfellows to myriad surgical operations that butchered it into countless fragments. My generation of scholars encountered a 'Humpty-Dumpty' Bible. The new scholarship that marked the end of the last two millennia and the beginning of the present one valiantly picked up these pieces, and have been more successful 'king's horses and men' – but the cracks still show. It remains difficult, even after three decades of narrative approaches to the text, to refer unselfconsciously to the Genesis creation story, for example, and not instinctively block one's ears to the reflex question – which one? – while remaining immune to the accusation of some kind of religious fundamentalism.

Thematic readings of particular biblical books, and of collections of books, have brought new levels of meaning to the fore, as well as the creative skills of biblical writers who were responsible for the texts we have inherited (Alter 1981; Alter and Kermode 1987; Clines 1997; Gunn 2000). This thematic process is often one of rediscovery in identifying links and patterns that had been recognised in earlier centuries by pre-critical scholars, including generations of rabbinic and patristic writers. In their book, *Gender, Power, and Promise*, Fewell and Gunn, with carefully chosen examples, take us through the biblical narrative from Genesis to Kings and, by so doing, clearly identify a unifying discourse. This discourse they term 'the first great story of the Bible' (1993: 12), which extends from creation to the fall of Jerusalem and the exile of Judah. Biblical scholars had previously grouped these texts together and used technical terms, such as the 'hexateuch', the 'octateuch' or the grouping isolated in Fewell and Gunn's study, the 'enneateuch', to describe them (Eissfeldt 1965: 136, 156). Scholars working from the hermeneutical stance of historical criticism identified these various groupings of texts, recognising amongst them common source material. This provided a means for them to distinguish types of literary genre, together with possible 'Sitz in Leben' for the material, and, they believed, sufficient evidence to trace back to the 'Urtext' that had been overlaid and hidden by the hands of editors down the centuries. As we noted in the previous chapter, these scholars, invariably white, western and male, lost sight of the finished model in their endless search for the earliest particle, the first building brick of biblical tradition. Their idolatry of historicism deluded them into believing they were objective scientists, and not subjective gendered and enculturated individuals with beliefs and non-beliefs that might inform their project. This point is directly and powerfully expressed by Walter Brueggemann:

> In my field of Scripture study, *historical criticism* has become a mode of silencing the text by eliminating its artistic, dramatic, subversive power. I do not wish to overstate my critique of historical criticism. It is, nonetheless, increasingly clear that historical criticism is no objective, disinterested tool of interpretation, but it has become a way to trim

texts down to the ideology of Enlightenment reason and
autonomy and to explain away from the text all the hurts
and hopes that do not conform to the ideology of objectivity.

(1992: 64–5; his emphasis)

In 'The Old Testament Histories', a chapter from *What Does Eve
Do to Help?* (1990), David Clines rediscovers the extended biblical
narratives and reclaims them from the source critics, referring to the
'enneateuch' as the 'Primary History' (after Freedman 1976). This
'Primary History', inclusive of Genesis through to 2 Kings, is largely
paralleled by the 'Secondary History', comprising eleven texts in all,
including 1 and 2 Chronicles, Ezra, Nehemiah and apocryphal/
deuterocanonical texts (1990: 90). Clines presents these two his-
toriographies as the central biblical metanarratives. The term
'histories' to describe these two sets of texts is misleading to the
modern reader, who may assume that history means factual accounts.
Clines, in sympathy with his biblical authors, is using the term
simply to mean 'narrative sequences' (1990: 91), loosely held
together by common families, gods and time-frame. In drawing
attention to the 'fundamentally different outlooks on the past' –
often a shared past – owned by these 'histories', Clines divulges how
the Bible in itself undermines modern historiography. There is not
just one account of this 'history' of the God of Israel's dealings with
his people and their neighbours – there are two possibilities. Casting
a glance in the direction of Christianity's early 'history', the same
tendency is clearly seen in very different presentations of Jesus'
person and mission in the canonical four Gospels.

Clines sums up the narrative of 'Primary History' to be about 'fair
beginnings and foul endings' (1990: 93). In this chapter and the
next we will explore this 'Primary History', and attempt to explain
how the major biblical aim is accentuated throughout. That aim,
shared by the biblical authors, is to show that, however fair the
beginnings or foul the endings, God's omnipotence shines through
even the messiest of human lives.

LAWS ARE MADE TO BE BROKEN

This truism sums up a strategy evident in feminist hermeneutics
and characteristic of 'deconstructive' criticism. This strategy incor-
porates a methodological approach to texts that reads them 'against
the grain', employed from a 'hermeneutics of suspicion' standpoint.

It looks behind a statute or teaching to uncover the context that *prompted* it (Fiorenza 1984: 15ff.; Brooten 1985). Thus, when the author of 1 Timothy forbade women to teach, feminist exegetes uncovered the unconventional women and their lifestyles that prompted this prohibition and challenged it by persisting in being a 'thorn in the flesh' in the process of conformity evident in certain manifestations of Christianity in the early centuries – and beyond (Gössmann 1999). Once a teaching is revealed to be relative, applying only to a particular context, and cannot be remotely relevant outside it, then the authority of the teaching is destabilised. Any God with affinities with the aspirations of feminism would indeed encourage any such teaching or law to be broken.

A version of this process is discernible and active within the biblical text itself. In the Torah the law codes present prescribed roles for men and women, but the narratives, particularly in Genesis, consistently challenge and undermine those roles. The nature of the relationship between biblical narrative and biblical law has been investigated and debated by generations of scholars who present a vast range of hypotheses, usually supported by various permutations of Wellhausen's multiple source theory. If we work with the text in its final form, then the conscious links between law and narrative intended by those authors/editors who gave this literature its definitive literary shape emerge organically, or naturally. Such a holistic approach to the text allows for the identification of the theme of *demasculisation* that is consistently evident in Genesis and elsewhere in the biblical narrative. Furthermore, by examining it in relation to the biblical law codes, we can divulge further the all-extensive character of divine power that was most forcefully introduced in Genesis by the concept of *imago dei.*

As we discussed in the previous chapter, as well as containing the cultic regulations for the building, staffing and rituals associated within the Temple/Tabernacle, the biblical law codes prescribe familial, social and religious behavioural patterns for an ancient Near Eastern, agrarian and patriarchal society. This society's structures are stable with clear set boundaries for all its members – from livestock to wives and children. At the heart of it lies the family unit headed by a patriarch. It is flexible in that the laws can apply to an extended family of three generations with adult children, or a 'nuclear' family of two generations of parents and children. The head of the family can exercise ultimate control over his household, and has the power over life and death in the case of adulterous wives (Lev. 20.10), or daughters who are accused of losing their virginity outside marriage

(Deut. 22.13–21). The absolute nature of this power is evident in the family law concerning the case of a rebellious son (21.18–21) and, in this extreme circumstance, both parents are expected to appear as plaintiffs before the court of elders. The parents' description of the rebellious son's behaviour, 'This son of ours is stubborn and rebellious. He will not obey us. He is a glutton and a drunkard' (21.20), presents us with an understanding of 'family' as a hierarchical unit, with senior members having the right in law to expect their adult offspring to behave according to their standards. The text continues, 'Then all the men of the town shall stone him to death' (21.21), and similar dire consequences await offspring that would strike or curse a parent (Exod. 21.15, 17; Lev. 20.9). Such a judgment puts a particular emphasis on the consequences of the fifth commandment rather than its imperative: 'Honour your father and mother, *so that your days may be long* in the land that the Lord your God is giving you' (Exod. 20.12; see also Deut. 5.16). From our standpoint these law codes can be regarded as comparatively enlightened when set beside, ancient Greek and Roman law (for example, the Twelve Tables in Roman law), particularly with regard to the concern expressed for the welfare of slaves and animals. Undoubtedly, however, they do represent a society that gives primary position to the father figure, with the rest of the household, especially its female members, only existing in relation to him – as part of his property.

Even after death a husband can exert control over his widow by means of levirate marriage (Deut. 25.5–10). If a man has died and has no son, his widow is obliged to have sexual relations with her dead husband's brother. Any child that is conceived and born from this union is deemed to be the dead man's offspring. This ensures the continuation of a particular male line. Although the autonomy of a woman evaporates in such a context, the system of levirate marriage would offer an alternative to destitution – the fate for childless widows (as the scene at the beginning of the book of Ruth clearly demonstrates). Such women – neither virgins nor mothers – have no economic or social value to either their husband's or their father's family.

A woman's identity was totally dependent on the primary male in her life – first her father, and then, when he had negotiated a marriage contract for her, her husband. The position of daughters and wives serves to illustrate the power of the primary male in ancient cultures. In Israelite society, the total lack of autonomy of these women, apparent from examples of legislation that survive in biblical texts, divulges the centrality and all-encompassing power of the male heads of households. When we turn from the laws of that society to the narrative traditions we soon discover an anarchic situation where male supremacy is at best weakened and at worst ridiculed. These situations come about through pragmatic alliances that occur between the women in the narrative and the God of Israel.

To return to the Eden story we discussed in the previous chapter, contemporary theology and biblical scholarship have not only applauded and condoned the interpretation of the first couple's autonomous action as a 'fall upward', but have particularly focused on Eve as the hero who liberates humanity from the childlike existence set out in the Garden (Roberts 1992; Sawyer 1992). This decisive step away from patristic and subsequent Christian interpretations of Eve as the originator of sin and prime cause of the estrangement between God and his beloved Adam opened up the way for extensive re-evaluations of Eve's role (Trible 1978: 72–143). Studies that place Eve in the wider context of Genesis, rather than restricting her to Genesis 2–3, have demonstrated that her character sets a pattern for female behaviour – throughout Genesis and beyond:

> Too innocent to be evil, too guileless to be seductive, she is a child testing her boundaries, weighing her options, making her choices. She makes her decision independent from those who claim authority over her. From time to time, in the larger story that follows, we shall glimpse Eve's daughters following in her footsteps.
>
> (Fewell and Gunn 1993: 38)

Moreover, Eve sets a pattern for divine/female interaction that has particular implications for the role of men in biblical theology.

Mary Daly's feminist, and subsequent post-Christian, critique of biblical and Christian theology identified patriarchy as the prime cause of women's subordination and victimisation and prompted her famous maxim: 'If God is male, then the male is God' (1973: 19). Although this observation is clearly borne out in much biblical teaching as well as in traditional ecclesiastical structures, one biblical (and pre-Enlightenment Christian) theological theme stands in antithesis to this maxim and even prompts its rephrasing: 'If God is male, then the male is nothing'. Prior to stating her maxim Daly comments:

The widespread conception of the 'Supreme Being' as an entity distinct from this world but controlling it according to plan and keeping human beings in a state of infantile subjection has been a not too subtle mask of the divine patriarch.

(1973: 18)

Rather than narrowing down this particular critique of patriarchal religion and focusing on women as unique victims, as *the* Other in this scheme, we need to deconstruct the implications of a 'Supreme Being' theology for both women and men – and for our readings of the biblical text.

This biblical theme of women – the matriarchs in Genesis – challenging the boundaries has tended to shine out of the text in an era when western culture has, at least partially, embraced a feminist agenda. Feminist biblical and theological scholarship has understandably clustered around these texts. This attraction has worked to restrict the scope of contemporary feminist theology and, at times, has blinded it from asking more searching questions as to why these texts do in fact challenge the boundaries (see Chapter 1, this volume). The biblical law codes reflect an uncompromising construction of prescribed gendered behaviour, and set beside them are narratives that subvert them. Luce Irigaray's use of mimesis in exploring female subjectivity, where authenticity may lie more in the *parody* of objectified womanhood than in the male constructed model, resonates with the gender games apparent in biblical narratives (1985). These games apply as much to constructed masculinity as to femininity. By focusing on the female characters in these narratives feminist critique has often overlooked what happens to constructed masculinity.

ABRAHAM – THE MIMETIC PATRIARCH

The figure of Abraham represents in both Jewish and Christian traditions the patriarch par excellence. Ironically, though, it is only through the suspension of his autonomy – the subjection of his patriarchal authority – that he becomes a father at all. First, Sarai (as she is known at this stage in the narrative) assumes control, decides that Hagar should be a surrogate mother in her stead and instructs Abram (as he is known at this stage) to impregnate the slave girl. Second, after the fertile years of Sarai and Abram's relationship are over, God decides for Abram that the time is right for him to father a child with Sarai. Thus, the human impossibility of conception in advanced old age is overcome by superhuman means and God reigns supreme.

Long before we reach the resolution to the question of a son for Abram and Sarai, Abram's identity is redefined in familial terms when the clan deity usurps his father's authority over him. The Abrahamic narratives reflect an agrarian lifestyle where familial clans form extended kinship communities. When we first encounter Abram he is living in his father's house alongside his brother and other members of the family. Ironically, Abram's breaking free from his paterfamilias is not an experience of liberation. Instead, he enters into a more extreme version of filial bondage heralded by a divine call that takes the form of an adoption scene. God tells him to leave his father's house and he blesses him as a father blesses a son – wishing greatness for him and promising him protection (Gen. 12.2–3). In response to these promises we are told, 'Abram went, as the Lord had told him', then, 'Abram was seventy-five years old when he departed from Haran' (12.4). Here we find one of the most explicit and recurrent biblical themes, and one that takes centre stage in the Christian scriptures. This is the manifestation of absolute control matched by radical obedience epitomised in the father/son relationship, and this is the only relationship permissible with God: 'Is not he your father, who created you, who made you and established you?' (Deut. 32.6). Believers, male and female alike, are forbidden maturity and autonomy – in effect they are forbidden a self-identity.

The first story of the Bible can be read along similar lines and the dependency motif is evident in the parental-type relationship that exists between God and Adam. Even after he recognises a partner in Eve, Adam still does not grow up. When the first couple take their first steps towards autonomy, their way is blocked by the impromptu arrival of the disappointed and angry parent. The scene of confrontation with the parent – so vital for human coming of age – becomes a dismal display of shifting the blame: responsibility is dropped in the face of divine disapproval, and autonomy becomes a dream that is never realised. Although Eve succeeds in liberating her and Adam from the herbaceous playpen, the parental yoke stays with them – to rest most heavily, later in the Genesis narrative, on Abram's shoulders.

We have noted that Abram's call can be read in familial terms – natural family is exchanged for divine adoption – and now we need

to examine how this *deusfamilias* functions. After the account of
Abram's call from God, the narrative continues with the story of
Abram and Sarai's sojourn in Egypt. In this story Abram's behaviour threatens to compromise God's promise, at least as far as the
possibility of fathering a great nation with his current wife, Sarai.
As they approach Egypt Abram imagines a situation in which his
life could be at stake when the Egyptians see the great beauty of
Sarai and discover she is his wife. It would be far better, Abram
speculates, if she were to pretend to be his sister. We are not told
whether there was any real threat to Abram's life, but the Egyptians
certainly were impressed by Sarai, and she, Abram's 'sister', ends up
in the Pharaoh's house. As a result, Abram lived very well in Egypt:
'And for her sake he dealt well with Abram; and he had sheep, oxen,
male donkeys, male and female slaves, female donkeys, and camels'
(Gen. 12.16). There is an ironic element in this story. Abram's treatment of Sarai, passing her on to the Pharaoh who readily takes her
as his wife (12.15, 19), is echoed later in the narrative when Sarai
'gives' Abram to an Egyptian to sleep with. In that story the status
symbols reverse and the Egyptian becomes a slave, Hagar (Kramer
1998: 221). Her treatment at the hands of Sarai certainly presents
us with more than adequate revenge for Sarai's experience in Egypt,
but then the text is silent as to Sarai's feelings, both when she is
given as Pharaoh's wife, and when she is handed back to Abram. In
this part of the narrative we encounter a clear enactment of biblical
law in a wife's passive status as the property of her husband.
We should note that the role Abram plays during this incident in
Egypt is not what we might expect from a mature and pious
patriarch, and that here he is more comfortable playing the role of
sibling than protective and responsible husband. Indeed, although
biblical law might have been upheld in Sarai's silent acquiescence
in her husband's plan, the plan itself subverts the laws that forbid
adultery.

However, it is in the saga of ensuring suitable offspring for Abram
that his emasculation and, with it, his lack of autonomy, is most
evident. First, Sarai takes matters into her own hands and instructs
Abram to sleep with her slave-girl, Hagar. The words given to Sarai
by the author of Genesis in this scene underline Abram's passivity:
'You see that the Lord has prevented me from bearing children; go
in to my slave-girl; it may be that I shall obtain children by her
(אולי אבנה ממנה, literally 'perhaps I will be built up through her').
Then we are told simply, 'And Abram listened to the voice of Sarai'
(16.2).

Sarai's speech exposes the vulnerability of Abram's masculinity and it falls apart on two counts. First, she excludes him from the problem of her infertility and announces that her lack of children is nothing to do with her husband, but is the work of 'the Lord'. Second, in the absence of divine action to remedy this situation, Sarai has chosen a bedfellow for him to impregnate. Recently, particularly in the context of both feminist and womanist exegesis, attention has focused on the portrayal of Sarai's character in this scene, most obviously in relation to her treatment of Hagar as a possession that can exploited to the ultimate degree (Trible 1984; Williams 1993; Teubal 1993; Barton 1999). If we move the lens towards Abram, he too can be seen as the victim in the execution of the interests of both God and Sarai. He is childless because of a divine whim, and now he is to become a father through the services of a foreign slave-girl because, after being married for countless decades without one, his wife suddenly decides action must be taken to give her a child – not the easiest demand for an 86-year-old to obey (16.15).

The story of Hagar and her son Ishmael continues to be dominated by Sarai's interests; the role of fatherhood is denied Abram in the narrative, despite the arrival of his first-born son. God intervenes yet again, this time to assure Abram that the 'real' heir has yet to be born, but since he, Abram, has petitioned on Ishmael's behalf, this first son will prosper and be the father of nations (17.18–20). This reassurance comes in the context of God's revelation to Abram that Sarai, now renamed by God as Sarah, will produce a child, or rather, to quote the words given to God in this dialogue, 'I will give you a son by her' (17.16). Abraham, as he has now been renamed by God, is denuded of power at a rate commensurate to the acceleration of dynamic divine power released for the process of determining the birth of the elect nation. His role as father, as protector of his son, is usurped by God, along with his role as husband and primary instigator of his wife's pregnancy. The limitations of Abraham's identity as a patriarch are now clearly defined and subordinate to divine supremacy.

At the grand ages of a hundred years and ninety years respectively, Abraham and Sarah's offspring, postponed by divine manipulation, is now permitted to be born. No clear reason is given as to why no child had been born previously, but then for Sarah to have given birth during the usual span of female fertility would have dulled divine intervention. Like children, these adults are ineffectual in reproductive terms and, just as old people mimic the young in their dependent role, Sarah and Abraham are childlike in their receptivity of God's plan and its execution.

Although Sarah's reaction to the sudden womb-opening scenario is more adult than that of her husband, such incredulity is deemed out of order in the midst of divine megapower. It is during the scene with the three strangers, understood as a divine visitation, that Sarah, by eavesdropping, hears of her imminent confinement. Her bemused reaction to the idea inevitably infers yet another slight on Abraham's masculinity: 'So Sarah laughed to herself, saying, "After I have grown old, and my husband is old, shall I have pleasure?"' (18.12). The Hebrew for 'pleasure' here is עדנה, a word associated with the noun 'Eden', and in this context it would seem to mean sexual pleasure and, according to the rabbis, has the connotation of fertile female moistness (Alter 1996: 79). Its use here highlights the parody of the scene. For Sarah, the prospect of her old husband providing the sexual pleasure that will lead to the conception of a child is a huge joke, never mind the idea of her – an infertile, post-menopausal woman – giving birth.

Abraham and Sarah, then, are mere instruments controlled to fulfil God's plan for an elect people. Sarah's character, however, is allowed more expression of will. And this is because, as a woman, her assertiveness further undermines her husband's authority in the face of the super-macho power of the divinity. Only once in these narratives do we find Abraham assertive towards God. Ironically, this adult Abraham flexes his autonomy and questions the justice of God, but not when he has been ordered to sacrifice the most precious member of his own family – the son that was at last born to him and Sarah. Rather, Abraham chooses to petition God to save the inhabitants of Sodom and Gomorrah (18.16–33). This unique chink in Abraham's consistently passive mood in relation to his God serves to accentuate his meekly obedient response to the outrageous divine demand for Isaac's life later in the text. In their discussion of Abraham's acquiescence in the matter of Isaac's sacrifice, Fewell and Gunn refer back to this assertive Abraham who argues so persuasively for the lives of godless strangers, but is later silent with no speech at the ready to save his son (1993: 52–5).

The Akedah (the Binding of Isaac) is the most vivid expression in the Abrahamic narrative of emasculation being utilised as a religious/political tool. Having at last produced a son with his beloved Sarah, Abraham once again encounters his whimsical God. As we have seen so far in the narrative, Abraham's role as husband has been compromised, and he has been unable to be an adequate father for

Ishmael. This time his capricious father-God not only denudes him of his role as protector of his beloved Isaac, but bids him to abuse the trust this son has in him by slaughtering him. Elements within Christian and Jewish tradition might express wonder at the absolute faith of Abraham that propels him to obey this horrific command, but more recent reflections on this story often express horror towards the act itself, shifting the focus from Abraham's faith to the act of slaughter and the nature of the God who could conceive of such a test. Carol Delaney is one scholar in particular who has focused on the implications of this story for perceptions of the biblical God, and for the generations who have revered it, and the question remains for her:

> Why is the willingness to sacrifice the child at God's command the model of faith, rather than the passionate protection of the child? What would be the shape of our society had *that* been the model of faith?
>
> (Delaney 1998: 149)

In Jewish tradition, the midrashic interpretations of the Akedah significantly develop Isaac's role in the drama (Vermes 1973: 193–227). Isaac becomes the active participant in his own sacrifice and, in so doing, rescues Abraham from the horrific role of would-be child-killer – a role so briefly and chillingly described in the biblical narrative. Often this role-switch of active participant from Abraham to Isaac is explained in terms of early Christian influence (Lieu 1996: 78–80). In their search to find meaning for the death of Christ, inevitably, Christian interpreters were drawn to the story of Abraham and Isaac and read it as an archetype for the crucifixion. Likewise, Jewish commentators focused on the Akedah in order to show that the type of sacrificial imagery and theology being articulated by Christians was already anticipated in their own tradition.

Isaac as archetype for Christ, or the Christ-event as a pale reflection of the Akedah, is immaterial to the present argument; what we should observe is that, in the process of making Isaac the active rather than passive figure, Abraham's fatherhood is redeemed. This process offers us an insight into how the meaning of a biblical narrative can develop in relation to different political/religious contexts and, in doing so, can be utilised by divergent theologies. To speculate briefly, the decreasing lack of political autonomy in Israel, particularly from the late second century BCE, culminating in Pompey's capture of Jerusalem in 63 BCE, inevitably affected Jewish attitudes to divine power and leadership. The Akedah as interpreted in midrash allows for greater human cooperation in the divine plan in a context where divine omnipotence is, if only temporarily, masked by this-worldly superpowers. The transcendence of God in this period, secreted away to the seventh heaven, can be understood as a withdrawal from direct action in human affairs. God is no longer wandering around Mount Moriah providing alternative sacrifices. The greatness of God may still be a reality for the faith community, but this divine omnipotence is hidden for the present time, just as autonomy for the Israelite nation at that time remained an unrealised ideal. A disempowered nation reflects on a hidden God, but in the meantime the 'children' of God, left on their own, have to act for themselves. Isaac, then, takes the initiative and controls his own sacrifice.

However, in the small-scale autocracies of clan life portrayed in the biblical accounts of ancient Israel, where patriarchal power was absolute, we find theologies that mirror and then exaggerate such absolutism. In such a context, when attempting to describe God as a phenomenon beyond human experience, an obvious image to develop is the image of extreme patriarchal power. In this theology there is no room for 'real' human patriarchs. Although male power is clearly evident in human affairs, supported by social and political legislation, in the face of God male power is emasculated. In fact the presence of the law codes in biblical texts, endorsing human patriarchal society, serve to exaggerate the contrast between it and the theology of dependency so evident in the narratives. Abraham might be the patriarch affirmed by biblical law codes that reflect a patriarchal hierarchy for familial/social organisation, but in his dealings with God he is a child without any autonomy in regard to his life choices, even in terms of his marital relationship and his own offspring.

A deconstruction of the story of Abraham, based on the recognition of the biblical paradigm of absolute power, can provide the materials for a reconstruction that is more resonant with contemporary theologies than with those produced by societies in past millennia. The masculinity represented by Abraham offers a non-assertive maleness in stark contrast to the images conjured up by the term 'patriarch'. In being the 'anti-patriarch' or the 'mimetic patriarch', Abraham parodies the concept of human patriarchy and, in doing so, redefines masculinity or, at least, exposes its limitations and its nature of dependency. In this process it becomes clear that, just as there are a multitude of ways of being 'woman' – past and present, so also 'being male' is as fragmented an experience in antiquity as it is in our postmodern world.

JUDAH – HYPOCRITE OR VICTIM?

We have already mentioned the biblical legislation for levirate marriage (Deut. 25.5–10) and the account of Tamar and Judah in Genesis 38 is a story that both illustrates and challenges this family law. The story goes beyond a description of how levirate marriage might be practised, and reveals critical weaknesses and lack of integrity in the male guardianship of this precept. The key male figure in this story is Judah, a highly significant patriarch in the history of Israel whose tribe gave the name to the land that contains the holy city Jerusalem, and whose blood line leads to King David. In the context of the story in Genesis 38, he is one of the sons of Jacob, renamed Israel (Gen. 35.9–15), and Leah, and is already a patriarch himself with an established household and three sons. Judah is singled out in his father's final oration as a figure with a majestic future (49.8–12). In contrast, the female character Tamar is a young woman, a non-Israelite, who is given to Judah's eldest son Er as a wife: 'Judah took a wife for Er his firstborn; her name was Tamar' (38.6). This short sentence encapsulates the nature of patriarchal Israelite society – both the adult son and daughter-in-law are in total subjection to the senior male figure.

Tamar is destined to be the foremother of the royal dynasty, stemming from the house of Judah, and eventually founded by David. In filling this role Tamar is a pawn within the divine plan. But, although a victim in this story in terms of the treatment she receives from Judah, she actively cooperates and conspires within that sphere to bring about both her and God's desired outcome: the birth of male offspring. Although Judah wields his extensive powers at the beginning of the narrative, at its end he is revealed as a hypocritical and weak stooge. Although, with the broader picture in view, it is the biblical author's intention that we see God's hand at work, moving the play towards the desired birth of the divinely anointed Israelite monarch, in isolation this story can be seen as an exemplary illustration of female sagacity outwitting male presumptions. Reformist feminist commentators might be tempted to leave the critical enquiry at this point. The content of Tamar's story is problematic on a number of counts, in particular the account of her adoption of the guise of prostitute. In Tamar, however, we have a female biblical figure who takes charge of her destiny by manipulating the value system of a patriarchal society to meet her own needs, and who is ultimately vindicated for her actions.

If we remain with the story, but switch the focus from Tamar to Judah, shifting the feminist hermeneutical stance in a manner more appropriate for an essentially androcentric text, then we can take the exegesis a step further and enquire about the strategies at work in relation to male power. As we have seen, in biblical law the system for levirate marriage serves both to ensure the male line of a hitherto childless deceased man and to provide a place and role for the widow within her husband's family and household. In the account of Judah's family, he sets out to fulfil the expectations of the levirate system by instructing his second son Onan to have sex with Tamar, 'to raise up offspring for your brother' (38.8). When Onan also dies Judah, understandably, hesitates to instruct Shelah, his third and only remaining son, to attempt a second levirate marriage. Judah creates a potential victim in Tamar through directly challenging the levirate system. Tamar is not allowed to stay in her father-in-law's house and is sent back to her father's house to await Judah's summons. This decision places Tamar in a desperate situation and transforms her into a woman without status in a context where she can no longer truly belong. She is neither married nor unmarried, and the negotiation of remarriage is not an option for her father since his daughter is still attached to Judah's house. She is in 'no man's land' in terms of identity, both belonging and not belonging to either family (Bird 1989: 119–39).

This story is not a straightforward account of male power victimising a powerless woman, since this woman is redeemed through her own initiative, which ultimately proves to be in tune with divine will. The outcome of the story with the humiliation of Judah actually presents the central male character as the ultimate victim. Judah and his wife, known only as the daughter of the Canaanite Shuah (38.2, 12), had produced three sons. Two were already dead, and their deaths, according to the narrative, would appear to be related to their attempts to conceive a child with Tamar. Up to this point Judah had acted according to the law of levirate marriage. His society valued male offspring above all else. He had been blessed with three sons, but now two were dead, and the law required of him to place his only surviving son into the same relationship that had proved fatal for the other two. The reader does sympathise with Judah's dilemma, and with his act of sending Tamar back to her father's house, albeit with the apparent false promise to send for her when he felt the time was right for Shelah to have sexual relations with her. The text does not actually tell us that Judah was lying to Tamar, only that he feared, or thought (אמר), that Shelah, too, would die like his brothers: כי אמר פן־ימות גם־הוא כאחיו. This patriarchal society was victimising Judah by its demand on him to surrender his offspring.

In his sexual encounter with the prostitute on his route to Timnah to meet the sheepshearers, Judah was committing no crime, and the text attaches no value-laden language to this encounter. Although dangerous, prostitution (זנה) was a recognised, and not necessarily illicit, occupation throughout the ancient Near Eastern countries, and the prostitute was a 'liminal' character outside the social order rather than a criminal (Niditch 1979: 143–9). The activity of prostitution was forbidden, however, to women who were not prostitutes by occupation. Hence there is no problem with the activity Judah and the 'prostitute' engage in on the road to Timnah. It is only when it transpires that Tamar had been illicitly engaging in prostitution that a vital boundary is transgressed.

If we examine Judah's situation further, we discover that his encounter with the prostitute apparently leaves him the victim of duplicity. The prostitute, rather than being merely an anonymous commodity used for Judah's sexual gratification, tricks him into parting with his personal possessions in lieu of payment. Judah's embarrassment over his sexual encounter is made apparent by the fact that he sent his companion, Hirah, back to pay the prostitute and retrieve his possessions, and, moreover, by the sudden adoption of new language to describe the woman. She is no longer a זנה (prostitute), but a קדשה (temple prostitute). The common street prostitute becomes a socially acceptable cultic figure. Commentators have attempted to read this cultic figure back to the earlier scene of the wayside encounter, and thereby make almost respectable both Tamar's disguise and Judah's proposition (von Rad 1972b: 354–5). Such a reading is unconvincing, not least on account of Judah's total lack of respect and extreme directness in his initial approach to the prostitute: 'Come, let me come into you' (38.16).

In her treatment of this biblical example of 'the harlot as heroine', Phyllis Bird rightly understands the role-switch for Tamar from common prostitute to temple prostitute to be in line with Judah's fear of being made a figure of ridicule by the prostitute (1989). This is evidenced, first, by his sending Hirah in his stead to pay the agreed sum to the prostitute and retrieve his possessions, and, second, by his fear of being mocked by searching for her (38.23). Tamar has compromised Judah, even before the final confrontation scene. She has exercised power over him and, in doing so, has made him a potentially weak figure in readers' eyes. Ironically, this embarrassment pales into insignificance when the full measure of his foolishness is revealed.

The final scene completes Judah's public shaming when the daughter-in-law he would have consigned to the flames exposes him as the true source of her shame. His fault lies both in his prior condemnation of Tamar to a life of no identity, and in his immediate desire to have her burnt to death. Tamar is vindicated by the penitent Judah, and she is triumphant with the birth of male twins. Her personhood and status are redeemed and secured for her lifetime.

Feminist commentators are prompted to herald this story as a welcome and rare example of a biblical text that is biased towards a woman's perspective, and even subversive towards the misogyny displayed by men such as Judah (Bos 1988: 48–9; Bal 1987: 89–103). Without denying that this story does allow for such a positive feminist reading, despite its patriarchal bonus-style happy ending, we need to probe more deeply to expose the thinking that allows for such a 'pro-woman/anti-male' account. The climax of the story is the redemption of Tamar through her conception of two male babies, one of which, Perez, will be an ancestor of King David. Her redemption, therefore, conveniently dovetails with God's plan for Israel's future. Tamar's exposure of Judah as the hypocrite par excellence in this final scene is not the sum of his blundering and suffering. It begins much sooner with the loss of his sons and his attempt to thwart Tamar's contribution to the davidic lineage – a vital component in the divine plan. It continues with his weakness and stupidity in dealing with the 'prostitute' on the road to Timnah. Instead of decisively settling the payment there and then, he leaves himself open to blackmail. Therefore, in the process of this story human male attempts to control and act effectively within the plot are presented as ill-conceived and futile. *Demasculisation* of male characters once again serves to underline the omnipotent, omniscient deity.

How does the outcome of this story relate to the biblical law on levirate marriage? Although Judah initially is observant by giving Onan to the widow Tamar, he then undermines the law by withholding his third son Shelah from her and sending her away from his household. Her subsequent fear of remaining a non-person in societal terms and her desperate measures to remedy her plight illustrate well the dire situation women could face without the protection of the levirate marriage law. Through her action and its incorporation into God's plan the law is effectively surpassed. Tamar is not impregnated by her dead husband's brother, as the law requires, but by his father. Ironically, it is not by fulfilling the levirate law that Tamar's redemptive pregnancy comes about, but, instead, by Judah breaking another law, the law of incest: 'You shall not uncover the nakedness of your daughter-in-law: she is your son's wife; you shall not uncover her nakedness' (Lev. 18.15).

The prohibition, לא תגלה ערותה, is repeated. We might note that the same section of Leviticus also forbids a man to have sexual relations with his brother's wife – the very coupling that is ostensibly prescribed in the levirate law. However, Leviticus 18.16 presumes the brother is still alive, so that sexual relationship would be an obvious act of adultery. In our context the prohibition in Leviticus 18.15, against sexual relations between father and daughter-in-law, reads like a mocking reminder of Judah's stupidity and inadvertent lawless behaviour. This lawlessness, however, is not greeted by divine retribution, as is the case in Onan's pathetic attempt to outwit the demands of levirate marriage. In contrast, this incestuous coupling is blessed with male twins – double the desired outcome of levirate coupling, a first-born son to continue the name of the deceased man (Deut. 25.6). To try to account for this apparent blatant and yet unchecked case of breaking the 'forbidden degree' clearly stated in Leviticus 18.15, Jacob Milgrom suggests that the act between Judah and Tamar was 'an early form of levirate marriage' (1993: 181). The question remains, if he was a permissible candidate, why did Judah not offer himself as a surrogate husband when Er, or indeed Onan, died? Furthermore, this explanation is not convincing when we consider the shock effect of Judah's exposure. If he had simply fulfilled the levirate law, why did Tamar not reveal herself to him immediately after they had sex, or, indeed, why did she not simply request Judah to father a child for Er when the latter had died? Why would there have been the need for such risk and elaborate disguise? Dating the levirate law in Deuteronomy, the incest laws in Leviticus, not to mention the story of Judah and Tamar in Genesis, in order to try and harmonise the content of all three, does seem an impossible and misguided task. In all probability they all reached their recognisable shape within the same period – a time of great creativity matched by the pressing need to produce both a cohesive sacred text with a metatheology prompted by exiles and invasions, and the inevitable encounters with 'difference' that accompany them. With this picture of composition in mind, Tamar and Judah's story can be seen to serve the purpose of divulging the inexorable, relentless triumph of divine guidance. Correspondingly, it underlines the futility of male, human endeavour in attempting to follow an alternative course when prompted only by immediate human need and weakness. In this context God-given law is surpassed and the action justified through service to a higher purpose – the divine lawgiver can change the rules when he is playing the game.

Male autonomy, in religious terms, is a transitory reality that evaporates in the presence of a mighty God. Walter Brueggemann has drawn our attention to the stark inconsistencies evident in the various biblical portraits of God. Instead of performing contortionist exegesis to reconcile the 'dark' side of this deity with the God who is compassionate and loving, Brueggemann allows them to stand together, and can reflect with honesty on aspects of the biblical God that are unsavoury, to say the least: 'Yahweh's self-regard is massive in its claim, strident in its expectation, and ominous in its potential' (1997: 296). Such a deity inevitably shrinks manhood as conceived by even the most excessive forms of human patriarchy.

We can conclude with a glance towards the book of Job where we find so clearly this macho God. In the scene where the great father-God confronts Job, who had dared to question God's motives, a thunderous divine voice booms out of a whirlwind and interrogates Job, among other things, as to whether he can truss up the primeval monsters of the deep (40.15–41.34). This hard-God rhetoric serves the simple purpose of driving Job to his knees in humble repentance of his audacity in even questioning the justice of God. In this dramatic scene there is certainly no 'Dalyesque' male as God. Biblical theology collapses human masculinity – and there we can encounter a flaccid entity. Obviously, with the dawn of modernity, when the Enlightenment heralds the death of the father-God, man – or, more accurately, white colonial man – does come of age. The rest of humanity remains on its knees.

Derrida uses the term 'paleonymy' to describe 'the occasional maintenance of an old name in order to launch a new concept' (1981a: 71). This is the context in which we might understand Irigaray's use of mimesis in her strategy for women to reappropriate the feminine (1985: 76). The uncovering of vulnerable maleness in biblical tradition, with the ultimate representation in the Christian Bible in the crucified figure of Christ, can show that lack of autonomy is a common experience for men as well as women – an observation made by womanist critiques of feminist theology (Grant 1989). Although the biblical texts were no doubt written by men and for men, the maleness affirmed by them is complex rather than purely hegemonic, and they contain an overriding theology that affirms the deity largely at the expense of the autonomy of the male audience.

4

BREAKING THE
BOUNDARIES

In the previous chapter we looked at the Genesis narrative and discussed how stories contained in it reveal an ordered world that can be destabilised in order for God's purpose to be worked through. This has the double-edged theological impact of showing both that God maintains and controls his creation at all times, and that he can disrupt it at will. Human male autonomy, in particular, could be identified as a significant casualty in this process. In the present chapter this major biblical trend will be explored further by investigating more closely the biblical writers' use of the female heroic and anti-heroic as a literary device. Esther Fuchs has argued that the treatment of female figures in biblical texts serves the purpose of reinforcing the values and beliefs of a patriarchal society:

> This discriminatory treatment produces female portraits intended, among other things, to validate the suspicion that women's apparent impotence is nothing but a deceptive disguise, that underneath their vulnerable coyness lurks a dangerously calculating mind.
>
> (Fuchs 1985: 143)

While the text does serve to collaborate with such an estimation of women, if the broader question of gender is raised and the roles of men as well as women are examined, then such a patriarchal ideological reading becomes less convincing. Women are not portrayed as schemers and plotters only to allow men to shine out as heroic characters. Rather, female initiative serves to emasculate male actions. The male characters we observed in Genesis in the previous chapter are too easily manipulated by women, their wisdom is lacking, and their agency shrinks before the power of divine omnipotence. It is not patriarchy that is served by these stories, but theocracy. Through the stories and characters from the books of Judges and Ruth that we shall discuss in the present chapter, we can observe an intensification of this tendency.

JUDGES

The connected narrative of the books of Judges and Ruth, recognised by the second century BCE Jewish scholars who compiled the Greek Bible (subsequently adopted by Christianity), offers the reader dramatic and disturbing contrasts through the many vivid and haunting characters and settings. The role of God within this framework is particularly enigmatic, ranging from total absence to shadowy appearances, leading up to an ultimate finesse at the end of Ruth. The book of Judges offers many images of God's people stumbling along without divine guidance, making mistakes that have fatal repercussions, and exercising judgements without good counsel. The violence and stupidity portrayed by certain male characters represent the biblical nadir of human behaviour. Female characters do not fare better and, although they feature significantly throughout the narrative, they do so simply to illustrate a godless society – both as victims and as perpetrators of violence. This rich spectrum of behaviour patterns opened up to women within the Judges narrative offers the female characters in the subsequent book of Ruth full scope to act and change their destitute status and, of course, to be key players in God's plan.

Women in the book of Judges are allowed active roles that usually remain the preserve of men, including leadership and murder, and it is in Judges that we encounter the female arch-villain of biblical narrative – Delilah. Delilah's character is foreshadowed by Pharaoh's wife in Genesis 39 with her scheming and devious behaviour, and rivalled subsequently in the book of Kings by the anti-hero Jezebel (1 Kings 16ff.). These women do not necessarily do bad things that other female characters do not do – rather, they act without any alliance with the Lord God of Israel. These women are bad either on their own account or on behalf of some human agency, unlike characters such as Sarah, who persuades Abraham to banish Hagar and his son Ishmael to certain death in the wilderness, or Rebekah, who wilfully tricks half-blind Isaac into blessing his second-born rather than his first (Gen. 27). As Danna Nolan Fewell comments:

Delilah's identity is not bound to any man. . . . She conducts her love affair with Samson and her business affairs with the lords of the Philistines without any father, brother or husband acting as mediator.

(1992: 73)

And, we might add, with no God of Israel whispering in her ear.

In her study of daughters in the book of Judges, Mieke Bal identifies a structure in the text that revolves around female characters, and is achieved through the interweaving of three female killers (Jael, Delilah and the unnamed woman, in 9.53, who kills Abimelech) and three female victims, all unnamed (Jephthah's daughter, Samson's 'wife' and the Levite's concubine). Through recourse to the notion of displacement (from Freudian dream theory), Bal interprets the experiences of the victims, who share the identity of 'daughters', as primary, and the killers, who fulfil the role of their displaced mothers, as reactive players within a hopeless cycle of violence:

If we view the murderesses in the book as avenging mothers, the excess of violence attached to them becomes understandable. Since they avenge the excessive violence done to the daughters, their role has to be, in turn, displaced. But where repression covers oppression, violence cannot but increase.

(1990: 38)

Although such parallelism is tempting in terms of an explanation for female violence, such an interpretation can dilute the potency of the extremes of human behaviour presented in the text. In producing these 'mothers' who are caught up in acts of vengeance, Bal seems to want to resist the idea that women are initiators as well as victims of violence. The meaning of the text, the agenda of the writer, is political theology where the alternative to theocracy, or divinely instituted monarchy, is played out with its most terrible consequences. The tribes of Israel represent the fragmented world of factionalism, greed and gratuitous violence. Any hope in the form of unifying leadership, even that ironically represented by a woman, Deborah, is short-lived. The writer gradually amasses his evidence through the stages of the narrative and creates the cumulative effect of an anarchic world – a world bereft of divine guidance where human power is inexpertly asserted and the victims, male and female, innocent and guilty, pile up.

Bal's parallelism does bring to the fore these dual concepts of the female heroic and anti-heroic at play in the text. Rather than seeing the female characters in terms of the one vindicating, or avenging, the other, we should disentangle them and focus on the cumulative and anarchic effect achieved through them. The element of surprise is used consistently throughout Judges and the female characters are key players in delivering this effect. If we take, for example, the song of Deborah, we find a familiar female image for the audience – the readers or hearers – in the mother of Sisera awaiting the return of her son from battle:

> Out of the window she peered, the mother of Sisera gazed through the lattice; 'Why is his chariot so long in coming? Why tarry the hoofbeats of his chariot?' Her wisest ladies make answer, indeed she answers the question herself: 'Are they not finding and dividing the spoil – a girl or two for every man; spoil of dyed stuffs for Sisera . . .?'
>
> (5.28–30a)

The scene challenges the audience with the combating images of the anxious mother set alongside the horror of war, where women are simply listed among the merchandise to be looted by the triumphant mob. But the cruel irony of the preceding verses has already destroyed any possibility of comfort from the homespun image of Sisera's mother. We have been reminded already of her son's gruesome fate at the hand of another woman, Jael:

> He asked water and she gave him milk, she brought him curds in a lordly bowl. She put her hand to the tent peg and her right hand to the workman's mallet; she struck Sisera a blow, she crushed his head, she shattered and pierced his temple.
>
> (5.25–6)

Rather than Sisera looting a woman's body as a trophy of war, a woman has shattered Sisera's skull. The irony is horrific and it stuns the audience through a mimetic process that paradoxically overturns expectation: a woman's act of hospitality becomes a scene of human carnage. Throughout the modern period scholarship has struggled to come to terms with this blatant betrayal of the trust associated with any basic act of hospitality (Bal 1988a). Jael behaves as the female nurturer, but the guise slips and she becomes the bloody executioner. This scene is one that we might be tempted to use as an illustration of Irigaray's notion of becoming woman (see Chapter 1, this volume), where the familiar concept is adopted and then subverted. In this scene there is no female solidarity – no Ruth figure to provide solace for a mother who has lost her son. Instead, Sisera's mother is mocked by the women who are culpable of her son's murder.

The theological import of this scene, placed towards the beginning of the book, underlines the inescapable power and sovereignty of God. The Jael episode is the central cameo of Deborah's 'reign' as Judge. God has raised up Deborah to judge Israel – a choice that prompted later rabbis to speculate that the situation recounted in Judges must have been desperate, since no suitable man was available and the only option was a woman. On the contrary, and in line with the use made of female figures by God in narratives such as those found in Genesis, we can surmise that Deborah was not appointed through lack of a male figure, but rather she was selected to underline God's low estimation of human male leadership. Her appointment serves as a reminder of the persistent biblical theological agenda.

Later in Judges another female character is used to express the hopeless and anarchic nature of a world under the rule of men – a leadership that is characterised and maintained only through violence. Abimelech, the son of the union between Gideon and his Shechemite concubine, wanted to ensure that he remained the unchallenged heir to his father's leadership. He hired 'worthless and reckless fellows', went to his father's house and killed all his stepbrothers (9.1–6). This bloody coup descends into clan infighting, through the apparent whimsical intervention of God (9.23), and Abimelech meets his inevitable violent end at the hands of a woman – an anarchic act in an anarchic world. The reaction that the author of Judges accords Abimelech encourages us to understand that the use of a female character as a killer is a deliberate emasculatory tool:

> But a certain woman threw an upper millstone on Abimelech's head, and crushed his skull. Immediately he called to the young man who carried his armour and said to him, 'Draw your sword and kill me, so people will not say about me, "A woman killed him."'
>
> (9.53–4)

In this topsy-turvy world of Judges, controlled and yet not controlled by God, gendered behaviour patterns are once more turned on their head and a mighty warrior is ignominiously slain by a woman.

The downward spiral of violence and destruction continues, exacerbated by the Israelites' idolatrous behaviour that runs to a full list:

> The Israelites again did what was evil in the sight of the Lord, worshipping the Baals and the Astartes, the gods of Aram, the gods of Sidon, the gods of Moab, the gods of the Ammonites, and the gods of the Philistines. Thus they abandoned the Lord, and did not worship him.
>
> (10.6)

Such behaviour is a big mistake in biblical terms, and the Lord's revenge amounts to eighteen years of oppression before the people repent and plead for God's mercy. Once the 'foreign' gods have been put aside, the author of this text allows us a rare insight into the compassionate dimension of the divine nature: 'he could no longer bear to see Israel suffer' (10.16). This moment at once reassures the audience that, whatever may occur in the interim, things will turn out right in the end.

Another episode in Judges sets a familiar scene and draws the audience into known narrative territory, only to shatter their expectations by confronting them with sheer unimaginable horror. Once again, a male figure takes on the role of an anti-hero, and his attempt to make the right thing happen develops into the most stupid course of action recorded in the Bible. Modern scholarship has valiantly attempted some form of explanation or exoneration for Jephthah's behaviour. For example, informed by Middle Eastern architecture, Boling carefully reconstructs the scene in Judges 11 to show that an animal could easily be the expected first creature to meet one's eyes on returning home (1975: 208). The rabbis, however, conclude that human stupidity, or weakness, is the only credible explanation for Jephthah's vow and subsequent action and, in doing so, they stay close to a theological agenda that confronts any biblical account that might prompt the questioning of God's role (*Genesis Rabbah* 60.3; see also Valler 1999). Jephthah, the Gileadite, is presented in Judges as an outcast from his family who adopts the life of a brigand, attracting similar outlaws and gradually building a significant force amongst the Israelites. He takes on the Ammonites and dominates the northern territories, subduing the Ephraimites, their tribal rivals.

Like other such figures singled out in Judges as leaders in this period, such as Othniel (3.10) and Gideon (6.34), the spirit of the Lord comes upon Jephthah (11.29), signalling a divine sanctioning for his period of leadership. Immediately after this happens we are told that Jephthah vows that, if he is given divine power to defeat the Ammonites, he will make an offering to God on his return:

> whoever comes out of the doors of my house to meet me, when I return victorious from the Ammonites, shall be the Lord's, to be offered up by me as a burnt offering.
>
> (11.31)

Human sacrifice is presumed to be acceptable to Yahweh – a presumption that remains uncorrected in Judges. The obvious risk as to the identity of the victim who must fulfil this dreadful vow is soon realised when Jephthah's own daughter dances out to meet her victorious father. But biblical readers and hearers have been here before. We, like our fellow listeners in ancient times, immediately recall another potential scene of human sacrifice, and another father faced with the impossible dilemma of either betraying their faith in God or committing infanticide: 'the book of Judges rewrites Genesis' (Fewell 1997: 144). Like Abraham, the father in that situation, Jephthah does not for one moment entertain the option of not carrying out the killing. Indeed, unlike the account of Abraham, we are permitted some insight into Jephthah's own feelings of horror at the tragedy:

> When he saw her, he tore his clothes, and said, 'Alas, my daughter! You have brought me very low; you have become the cause of great trouble to me. For I have opened my mouth to the Lord, and I cannot take back my vow.'
>
> (11.35)

Again, unlike the case of Abraham where the sacrifice of Isaac is a divine whim, for Jephthah this is a tragedy that he has manufactured.

Does God's silence in this episode comprise acquiescence to the fatal vow, and by extension the breaking of his own commandment against child sacrifice? This is a question anticipated by the rabbis and dealt with through switching the focus away from God and onto the defective character of Jephthah. Valler summarises the treatment of the story in the rabbinic sources:

As true believers, they (the Sages) could not accept the possibility of any fault in the conduct of God, the very embodiment of morality. For that reason, the compilers of the Aggadah tried hard to impute wickedness to Jephthah and thus foil any possibility of placing the Holy One, blessed be He, in any connection with the terrible deed of offering up the daughter as a sacrifice.

(1999: 49)

According to *Genesis Rabbah*, Jephthah's unqualified vow was in itself evidence of his stupidity. Anything could have confronted him as he approached his house – even an unclean animal. Would he have presumed to offer that up to God as a fitting sacrifice?

> Said the Holy One, Blessed be He, to him: 'Then had a camel or an ass or a dog come forth, you would have offered it up as a burnt offering!' What did the Lord do? He answered him unfittingly and prepared his daughter for him.
>
> (*Genesis Rabbah* 60.3)

And so, because he has made a ridiculous vow that allows for the possibility of the most inappropriate sacrifice being offered up to God, God responds to Jephthah by presenting *him* with the most inappropriate sacrifice for him to offer.

The rabbis are aware of the comparisons and contrasts between this child sacrifice and the Akedah in Genesis 22, and their midrashic explanation into the 'mind' of God in both incidents emphasises divine 'innocence':

> I commanded not Abraham to slay his son, but rather Lay not thy hand upon the lad, to tell the nations of the world of Abraham's love, who did not withhold his only son for me, to do the will of the Creator. I did not tell Jephthah to sacrifice his daughter.
>
> (*Tanhuma Haksdum*, cited in Valler 1999: 63)

Issues of theodicy remain unanswered. God might provide an alternative to his beloved son for Abraham to kill and sacrifice, but what kind of God would want his followers to be prepared even to kill their children? And why victimise the daughter in the process of punishing the father? Why was no last-minute reprieve given to

Jephthah once it was clear that the dreadful deed was about to happen?

Just as the ancient rabbis fix their gaze on Jephthah and neatly bypass the issue of God's role in the slaughter of his daughter, so contemporary feminist scholars have vindicated divine implication in the crime by focusing on the figure of the daughter. Phyllis Trible's exegesis of this scene from Judges notes the absence of the divine but does not scrutinise it:

> But in the story of the daughter of Jephthah, no angel inter-
> venes to save the child. The father carries out the human
> vow precisely as he spoke it; neither God nor man nor
> woman negates it.
>
> (Trible 1984: 105)

Trible draws particular attention to the story's postscript, when we are reminded of the daughter's virginity and then told that the women of Israel commemorated her sacrifice every year; she comments, 'In a dramatic way this sentence alters, though it does not eliminate, the finality of Jephthah's faithless vow' (1984: 106). Like the rabbis, Trible makes Jephthah the culpable character: God is left alone as the passive bystander – an uneasy, and incredible, role for the Creator of the universe.

Feminist scholars are understandably drawn to the plight of this unnamed girl, whose fate is a caricature of the most extreme patri-archal culture portrayed in biblical texts – rivalled only by the account of the unnamed concubine we encounter later in the book of Judges. Not only have these scholars challenged the text, but, in encountering it, have had to confront centuries of exegesis that has marginalised female characters such as these women, detracting from the brutality dealt out to them by symbolising their suffering or justifying their slaughter. The most quoted comment in this vein, emanating from Alexander Whyte at the dawn of the twentieth century, stands as a monument to the sins of the fathers of modern biblical scholarship. He comments as follows on the women's annual commemoration of the sacrifice of Jephthah's daughter:

> [They] came back to be far better daughters than they went
> out. They came back softened, and purified, and sobered at
> heart. They came back ready to die for their fathers, and for
> their brothers, and for their husbands, and for their God.
>
> (Whyte 1905)

Jephthah's daughter is one of the most poignant figures in biblical narrative: unnamed, the ideal of filial obedience, the perfect sacrifice. Indeed, as the Christian commentators noted, in her virginal state and her mode of obedience she is the prototype of Mary of Nazareth (*Speculum humanae salvationus*, chapter v, cited in Beal and Gunn 1999: 639). The narrative itself leaves open the possibility for interpreting the figure of God as culpable – the one character able to negate the vow, or to offer an alternative, does not. Yet the commentators down the centuries and up to the present day consistently declare him innocent. There have been dissident voices. Voltaire, for example, cites the story of Jephthah's daughter as the primary illustration of the brutal primitive religion of the Bible with its *dieu sanguinaire* (*Dictionnaire philosophique*, cited in Beal and Gunn 1999: 640). Voltaire's criticism emphasises in particular the violence of the Hebrew Bible's religion. But it is Christianity that centres its entire theology on child sacrifice, and therefore allows comments such as that of Whyte to make theological sense. It is not the father in this story, or his context, that should be the focus of negative criticism, but the theologies that not only prompt the text, but subsequently endorse it in later centuries. If we look back to the story of Jephthah to see if there is evidence to vindicate God's passivity, we discover that the text does not offer much evidence of a non-interventionist God who is unable to act in the light of the free will given to his creatures. The narrative that immediately follows the account of Jephthah is that of Samson, and it begins with a proactive God who opens the womb of Samson's mother and sends an angel (מלאך־יהוה) directly to inform her that she will conceive.

The rabbis' exposition of Jephthah's sacrifice serves to extricate their God from his implication in the matter of child sacrifice – expressly forbidden in the Torah in the context of prohibitions against 'foreign' practices: 'every abhorrent thing that the Lord hates they have done for their gods. They would even burn their sons and their daughters in the fire to their gods' (Deut. 12.31; see also Deut. 18.10; Lev. 18.21, 20.2–5). Such restrictions do not apply to God, however. As we saw in the case of Ishmael and Tamar, the commandments regarding primogeniture and incest, respectively, provide no boundary for the deity's plans. In the case of Isaac, the impossibility of God permitting his sacrifice is not apparently at the forefront of Abraham's mind as he readily sets off to carry out God's instructions for the child's sacrifice.

Fewell and Gunn are two contemporary scholars who dramatically shift the focus away from the stupid and brutal father, and the barbaric culture he exemplifies, and, by doing so, immediately delve deeper into the meaning of this story, or rather the reasons behind its inclusion. They introduce their exposition with the simple comment, 'Judges 11 is the story of two abused children, a boy and a girl' (1993: 126). They are perceptive in recognising that there is more than one victim and that blame cannot be assigned too readily. They make the point that the daughter would most likely have been aware of her father's crazy vow – vows were made publicly – and that the story's audience would know that she was thus aware (1993: 127). The daughter has an element of control over her fate, demonstrated by her subsequent choice to spend her remaining days with her women friends. Her actions, not her passivity, focus attention on the foolishness of her father. Once again a woman is used to show up the vacuum of wisdom and mature leadership when men and not God are in control. When God chooses to remove himself from Israel's activities, an anarchic world emerges – a child dies and a nation diminishes through the carnage of intertribal warfare. When he chooses to intervene, a child's life is saved and a nation is born.

Women in the book of Judges play out various literary devices, for example they parody their male counterparts, as leaders and killers. As such they scandalise the would-be heroes, such as Abimelech (see p. 69), who pleads in death to his young armour-bearer, 'Draw your sword and kill me, so people will not say about me, "A woman killed him"' (9.53–4). Jael's act is also given great emphasis in Deborah's song of victory:

> She put her hand to the tent peg and her right hand to the workman's mallet; she struck Sisera a blow, she crushed his head, she shattered and pierced his temple. He sank, he fell, he lay still at [בין] her feet; at her feet he sank, he fell; where he sank, there he fell dead.
>
> (5.26–7)

The repetition of the verb נפל (*he* fell) and the phrase בין רגליה (between *her* feet) emphasises male power collapsed by female initiative – a horrific irony from the perspective of the male writers and audience. This is noted in Alter's excursus on this passage from the Song of Deborah (1983: 615–37), which presents the

> image of the Canaanite general felled by the hand of a woman, lying shattered between her legs in a hideous

parody of soldierly assault on the women of the defeated foe.

(633)

Sisera's mother's image of her son enjoying the subjection of the enemy's women is utterly subverted by this dramatic switch of gender-play.

A similar irony is evident in the fate of Samson who, despite his eventual heroic death, is emasculated by having his hair shaved off at the instigation of Delilah (Judg. 16.18–19). Samson – like Sisera, like Lot (Gen. 19.30–6) and, most horribly, like Holofernes in the book of Judith (13.1–9) – makes the mistake of falling asleep in the presence of a female with intent.

But, just as the author of the book of Judges uses women to illustrate anarchic violence against men, he also employs them as a literary device to illustrate the nadir of male behaviour. We have discussed how a father gets himself into an unimaginable trap, and how this extreme example of male lack of foresight leads to a young woman's slaughter. This, however, is only a foretaste of the horror that unfolds in the story of the Levite's concubine (פִּילֶגֶשׁ) that is recounted towards the end of the Judges narrative. There are many enigmatic features in this story, including the stark style in which it is recounted, the relationship between the Levite and his פִּילֶגֶשׁ, the attitudes to male sexuality implicit in the account, and the story's wider political context. All these issues are discussed in detail by recent commentators – Soggin (1981), Niditch (1982), Trible (1984), Bal (1988b), Fewell (1992), Brenner and van Dijk-Hemmes (1993), Brenner (1999) and Fewell and Gunn (1993), to name but a few. The purpose in looking at this story here is to focus on the role/non-role of the deity in the events that unfold, and try to discover the theological agenda that prompts its inclusion within the Judges narrative.

The opening words in the story of the Levite's concubine are part of a recurrent phrase in the book of Judges. This appears in full in 17.6 and also in 21.25 where it functions as the concluding words to the entire Judges narrative: 'In those days there was no king in Israel; all the people did what was right in their own eyes' (see also 18.1; 19.1). The phrase explicitly laments the lack of kingship and implicitly yearns for a divinely appointed ruler who will be the instrument of God, ruling Israel, his elect people – a hope that will be fulfilled by David's eventual accession. By opening the account of the Levite's concubine with the words, 'In those days there was no king in Israel', the author is not simply stating the obvious and pointing to the lack of any monarchy, but implicitly indicating the lack of divine control. A king would be a phenomenon that could only exist for Israel if God had instigated the reign. If there is no king, and moreover not even a judge whom God has temporarily anointed with his spirit, then God is not active – we have spiralled downwards, even further than in the episode with Jephthah, who was imbued with God's spirit for a time. The phrase thus signals to the audience that we have reached a totally desolate time and we are in a situation that is utterly without hope.

The story in Judges 19–20 recounts how the woman, the unnamed concubine, is sent out of the house where she is staying for the night, and is gang-raped throughout the night by the men of Gibeah, the place where she and her partner had stopped to break their journey back to Ephraim. We are told that, by the morning, she had managed to stagger back to the house where she and her partner were staying, and had collapsed on the threshold. We are not told whether she is actually dead at this point, although in the next chapter the Levite claims 'they raped my concubine until she died' (ענו ותמת) (20.5). The woman is then mutilated by her partner who butchers her body into twelve pieces to be sent out to all the land of Israel as a macabre symbol of the fragmented state of Israel's tribes. The Levite is affronted that one tribe, the Benjamites, should have perpetrated such a crime against a member of the Levite tribe, setting brother against brother. Israel is broken. Thus the focus of the story shifts from the act of violent rape to the identity of the rapists.

This story was one of the 'lost' tales of the Bible – one too horrific to be dealt with other than symbolically by commentators down the centuries, and left unread by priests and ordinary people. Feminist scholars were at the vanguard of retrieving and confronting this biblical horror story. Their exegesis focused on the figure of the woman, rather than the political and military issues that form the background of the account. In thus switching the focus, this unnamed woman's story was brought to the fore and her fate mourned anew. Furthermore, the meaning of this story within its present context, a story about sexual violence, was confronted and not lost in speculation about the symbolic meanings.

The problem of dealing with the existence of such a brutal account of male behaviour in a sacred text is compounded by the absence of divine intervention. God is once again silent and passive in this scene, as he was when Jephthah slaughtered his daughter. Again, as in the case of Jephthah, there is a parallel story in Genesis – this time with Lot as the central character, rather than Abraham (Gen. 19). Rather than focus on reconstructing some non-extant foundational account that might have formed the basis of the stories in Genesis and Judges, we are prompted to compare and contrast them as they stand. Their mutually reflective existence in Genesis and Judges is almost like a deliberate literary device on the part of the authors/editors who gave these texts their final form. Both sets of stories stand in mimetic relation to one another – Abraham and Isaac with Jephthah and his daughter, and Lot and his daughters with the Levite and his concubine – and serve to signal the presence and absence of God.

In the Genesis account a divine presence serves to oversee the protection of both the male guests and the women. In the same manner in which an angel provides the substitute sacrifice in Genesis 22, so the two angels in Genesis 19 physically rescue Lot – and his daughters – from the mob. In Judges there is no divine presence to ensure a substitute for Jephthah's daughter, nor are angels present to protect the Levite's concubine from being gang-raped. In Genesis 19 and Judges 19 a scene of hospitality is interrupted by a local gang who demand the guests be sent outside the house to be raped. In both stories the rape of women is seen to be the lesser evil to the rape of men, and the women of the house are offered up instead – Lot's daughters in Genesis and the daughter of the house and the female guest in Judges (Stone 1996: 69–84). In Judges the mob are apparently satisfied with one woman – the guest: 'they wantonly raped her, and abused her all through the night until the morning' (19.25). In Genesis the mob violently reject the offer of female substitutes and try to seize Lot himself (19.9), but the angels intervene and strike the mob blind. Ultimate divine censure then follows, when God himself engages in the total destruction of Sodom and Gomorrah by raining down fire and brimstone (19.24–5).

Such a powerful scene, where divine forces protect the innocent and wreak vengeance on the perpetrators, stands in antithesis to the lonely woman in Judges who is raped, murdered and mutilated with not one word of concern, compassion or sorrow allowed to be uttered on her behalf. Her fate, though once hidden and forgotten, is mourned by commentators today. Phyllis Trible (1984) and Mieke Bal (1988b), in particular, have recovered this anonymous victim and made her story a familiar one to recent generations of biblical readers. Whilst inevitably haunted by this female figure and her fate,

our central concern in this volume lies with the theology that under-
lies these stories. The accounts of Jephthah's daughter and the
Levite's concubine serve to illustrate a godless land. The key difference between the literary contexts of Genesis and Judges lies in the
role given to the deity. Fewell argues that the deity has been rejected
by Israel:

> God had been abandoned so many times by Israel and
> remembered again only when the people are under major
> threat that, by the time of Jephthah, God has grown im-
> patient with the troubling of Israel (10.16 . . .). Yahweh
> is merely another party to be bargained with and, once
> the victory is granted, to be dispensed with, like the
> daughter.
>
> (1992: 71–2)

This would then account for God's steady withdrawal from the
scenes recounted in Judges. This passive role for God is underlined
by the repeated refrain, which laments the absence of a king, and
which is given such careful positioning in the book. It makes its
first appearance in the heart of the book, as Israel's downward spiral
starts to reach its nadir, and is deliberately at its end as a summary
and conclusion to the terrible events described. It is not the acts or
non-acts of Israel that are effective – they are not the main plot. It
is the ruthless momentum throughout Israel's history of God's plan
– of God's will being done – that provides meaning for the events
in Judges. It is not through Israel's initiative that a king will reign
– it is God's action that will bring it about. This divine plan includes
the messy scenes that deal with Saul, the decoy king, and it begins
before the advent of David with the opening-up of Hannah's womb
to instigate the birth of Samuel, who is destined to be the one who
will anoint David. Such accounts of divine omniscience and omnipotence cannot allow for God's presence to be subject to Israel's
attitude. The absence of God in the latter scenes of Judges has to
be the 'choice' of God. Only that explanation is credible in the light
of biblical theology. God might be cajoled at times (10.6), but
clearly not at others. Action is dependent on the unknown ways
of God and not on the perceived needs of Israel. From human perspective this means experiencing inconsistency in terms of divine
intercession, but it bears witness to the 'unknowable-ness' of God –
a consistent biblical theme.

RUTH

The canonical order of the Septuagint, adopted by Christianity, makes the Bible's political/theological agenda more explicit. Taking up the story from the end of the book of Judges, where we had reached the nadir of the downward spiral of death, destruction and desolation, characterised by the absence of God, we next encounter the book of Ruth. Judges prepares us for the introduction of the three widowed characters at the story's outset, ensuring that we know we have met them in a world that is a very dangerous place for vulnerable women. More explicitly, Naomi and Ruth head for Bethlehem as their one hope of a place for survival and restoration. But the readers who have just concluded the Judges narrative are immediately aware that Bethlehemites were the people who populated Gibeah (Judges 19.16). Such men had gang-raped a woman and left her for dead, despite the fact that she was accompanied by her 'husband'. Naomi and Ruth are venturing into this place without any such protection. The clue to their survival in the face of such potential danger lies in the possibility that the God who had absented himself in the concubine's story might be present for Naomi and Ruth. The story of Ruth is an excellent example of a biblical text that subtly but relentlessly expresses biblical ideology through twining the motifs of the 'hidden' God and the female hero. Both are used as literary tools to assert the theology of divine omniscience, and the story encapsulates the promise of redemption. God's gradual re-emergence coincides with the transformation from famine to plenty, from barrenness to fertility.

The impact of recent literary study on the Bible has indirectly resulted in the suppression of the biblical theocratic agenda, through scholars' attempts to 'rescue' stories from the Bible and recontextualise them in the milieu of 'secular' folklore. However, while we might wonder at such a naive separation of the religious and 'secular' – a post-Enlightenment concept alien to the ancient world – these literary investigations have inadvertently highlighted the subtleties of biblical theology. For example, Jack Sasson's application of the theoretical work of Vladimir Propp to the text of the book of Ruth meant that the critical lens moved to focus on the pre-biblical context of elements of the story and its genre as a folk tale (1989). God's background role in the tale prompted assumptions that the book of Ruth's religious or theological content was insignificant, perhaps artificially and unconvincingly grafted on to ensure its inclusion in the Hebrew canon. Sasson comments that the opinion of

Lucien Gautier, 'of almost a century ago on this matter is still relevant: "Au point de vue religieux, la portée du livre de Ruth est à peu près nulle."' (1989: 249). Sasson dismisses the notion of the 'hidden God' at work in the narrative:

> we would like to buttress our criticism of such an approach by returning . . . to our analysis of *Ruth* as a folktale in model. From that discussion, it should be clear that those episodes most often cited as activated by a 'hidden' God fit neatly into Propp's scheme of sequential function. . . . Finally, we should like it to be recalled that no *character role* needed to be assigned to God, another testimony to the relatively inconsequential nature of his involvement in the narrative.
>
> (1989: 221)

In the foreword to the second edition of his study of Ruth, Sasson does revise this stance:

> I wrote about the marginal value of Ruth for our understanding of Hebrew theological ideology or religious convictions. I think I was then insensitive to the manifold issues and perspectives that the topics raise. . . . I should have distinguished between the religious and the theological in Ruth and then also realised that these categories play differently whether Ruth is assessed as an independent tale or as part of sacred scripture. Had I been alert to these distinctions, I would certainly have refrained from blanket censure of efforts to uncover the workings of a providential God.
>
> (1989: xv)

Such a self-critical stance that welcomes the inevitable momentum of biblical studies is refreshing to read. Sasson does persist, however, in assuming that Ruth could be assessed as an 'independent tale', a position that many contemporary scholars would contest, myself included, since our only experience of Ruth is as a text within the Hebrew and Christian canons – an uncontested religious and theological context.

Another contemporary approach to biblical studies that loses sight of the powerful theocratic agenda motivating, albeit often implicitly, the presentation of the book of Ruth is feminist analysis. Like the literary analysis applied by Sasson, feminist analysis can lose sight of the 'wood' by focusing on the 'trees'. In Sasson's case the 'trees' were the match between folklore, or fairy tale, personae and the characters in Ruth, which masked any vision of the 'wood', namely God. In the case of feminist analysis the 'trees' are the powerful central female characters and, again, the 'wood' is the role of the deity (for example, Brenner 1993). Both types of analyses take the text out of its biblical context and allow the characters to perform independently of the dominant agenda. André LaCocque makes a similar criticism of Phyllis Trible's exegesis of the book of Ruth:

> Phyllis Trible has transposed a modern problematic into a Second Temple period story. She sees in the text the war between the sexes, while the opposition here is not between males and females per se, but between what they represent in the conflict between ideologists and utopians in Jerusalem.
>
> (1990: 113)

For LaCocque the book of Ruth functions on a variety of levels. Within its immediate historical context, which he dates to the Second Temple period, it offers a political teaching that advocates a radical revision of Israel's xenophobia in the light of the positive attitude to 'foreign' marriage. In a wider context, it belongs with other biblical texts that also present subversive female figures who become key divine agents – Susanna, Judith and Esther:

> All four are living demonstrations of the ineptitude of the institutionalised answers to adversity. . . . Where the 'institution' fails, the 'event' must take its place. It is then made clear that God opts for the unexpected, the unconventional, even the extravagant; first in the choice of his agents, then in the choice of means by which these will bring about Israel's liberation.
>
> (LaCocque 1990: 118)

The theological agenda is subtly contrived in the book of Ruth, where events gradually move forward, gently prodded by fatalistic encounters that climax with the birth of a son, Obed. This son is described by the chorus of women, who function as the theological informants on the plot, as having been 'born to Naomi' (4.17). Even though the birth would seem unremarkable in the sense that a couple, Ruth and Boaz, come together and conceive a child, the text transforms this 'normality' by identifying the child as Naomi's – a miracle birth to a childless widow. The miraculous undercurrent to Obed's birth is recognised and made explicit in rabbinical commentaries and, along with other such births, is seen as an essential ingredient of the divine plan, a point picked up by Rachel Adler:

> The barren woman is useful because she proves God's fertility, so to speak. Hence midrashim from the talmudic to the late medieval collections industrially multiply the number of barren women in the Bible and dramatize the miracle of their conception. According to a talmudic midrash (b.Yebamoth 64b), Sarah has no womb. Numbers Rabbah explains that the angel who appeared to Samson's mother was careful to inform her that it was she and not her husband who was the barren one (Naso 10.5). According to Resh Lakish in Ruth Rabbah 6.2, Ruth was forty years old when she became pregnant and had Obed as a miracle. In Ruth Rabbah 7.14, moreover, he asserts that Ruth, too, lacked the main portion of her womb.
>
> (1977: 244)

As the story unfolds, Naomi's and Ruth's predicament changes from destitution to restoration, and a cursory reading of the text would allow the reader to conclude that this is apparently the result of the women's astute actions coupled with Boaz's cooperation. But this illusion of human agency evaporates in the final section, when the chorus of Bethlehemites, in stark contrast to the crowd of them encountered in Judges 19, reveals the real context for these events in their eulogy on the marriage of Ruth and Boaz:

> May the Lord make the woman who is coming into your house like Rachel and Leah, who together built up the house of Israel. May you produce children in Ephrathah and bestow a name in Bethlehem; and, through the children that the Lord will give you by this young woman, may your house be like the house of Perez, whom Tamar bore to Judah.
>
> (4.11–12)

Just as Tamar's trickery was permitted to ensure the right progeny was born, so Ruth and Boaz's coupling is at God's design (see

Chapter 3, this volume; Ellen van Wolde also discusses the semantic relationship between the stories of Ruth and Tamar (1997: 426–51)). The genealogy placed at the very end of the book of Ruth concludes with the revelation that Obed will be King David's grandfather. From the book of Genesis to that of Ruth, God's control ensures that the correct line of ancestors is in place for the advent of his chosen leader for Israel. The ascendancy of the female characters in the book of Ruth allows the redemptive role played by Boaz to be diluted, and this motif is finessed by the climactic birth of Obed:

> Naomi took the child and laid him in her bosom, and became his nurse. The women of the neighbourhood gave him a name, saying, 'A son has been born to Naomi.' They named him Obed; he became the father of Jesse, the father of David.
>
> (4.16–17)

God's hand is revealed and, furthermore, the transference of the child to Naomi effectively removes both Ruth and Boaz from the scene. God has provided a son for Naomi, and the Lord who had 'emptied' Naomi (1.21) has now restored her through the birth of Obed (4.15).

Fewell and Gunn draw attention to the centrality of Naomi in the book of Ruth, and show convincingly that Ruth's devotion to Naomi is far from reciprocal (1988). Like Tamar, Naomi needed a son to provide an identity for her and to give purpose to her life. Her desperation is clearly articulated in the opening chapter. She discards the attempts by Oprah and Ruth to provide support – only a husband and sons have any worth for her. She reluctantly accepts Ruth's company and, once in Bethlehem, immediately sets about engineering a real use for Ruth as bait for Boaz – a male relative who can perform a levirate task (see Chapters 2 and 3, this volume). In fact, in going a step further than the prescribed levirate means of gaining a child for a dead man, Naomi uses a surrogate female as well as a male. In the story of Tamar, God's plan allows the boundaries of incest to be broken through an alternative, unlegislated, form of levirate coupling. In the story of Naomi, the levirate legislation is compromised once more, this time by allowing Ruth to stand in for the post-menopausal Naomi – a variation on the miracle of older women conceiving, which was introduced in Sarah's story. The common strand running through these stories is that, despite dire situations that would thwart any human machinations,

God is at work ensuring the right sons are born in his selected line of descent – all bear witness to the totality of divine power and control.

In the book of Judges, Mieke Bal (1990) finds material for understanding the complexity of biblical patriarchy, or patriarchies. This complexity intensifies if we include the book of Ruth and its portrayal, and partial subversion, of patriarchy. By recognising the plurality of patriarchal systems, the process of their deconstruction then becomes more viable. But the Bible is not about humanly constructed political and social systems. Human leadership is measured solely in terms of a leader's allegiance and obedience to the deity and, throughout the books of 1 and 2 Kings, a king's lifetime achievements can be neatly written off by the frequently used authorial comment, 'did evil in the sight of the Lord'. In the ninth century BCE Israelite King Omri was one the nation's most powerful rulers. Credited with capturing Moabite lands according to the extra-biblical evidence of the Moabite Stone, his deeds prompting Assyrians to call Israel the 'land of Omri' long after his death, he is merited with seven verses by the biblical commentator (1 Kings 11.21–8). Patriarchal systems were a fact of life in the ancient world, and the variety of social and political organisation represented by them obviously would affect the experiences of all men, women and children therein. The Bible, as a collective product of a variety of such systems, likewise reflects a range of experiences and possibilities for its various characters. The Bible does not, however, offer a human system of government that is ultimately viable.

If we turn to the Christian Bible, this observation is equally valid. Even taking into account the evidence from the Gospels that record Jesus of Nazareth teaching his contemporaries to render to Caesar what is Caesar's, or St Paul exhorting his audience to be obedient to the governing authorities that have been instituted by God (Rom. 13), humanly ordained systems are transitory. In the case of the teaching of Jesus and Paul the context is one of imminent eschatological expectation – believers should remain obedient in the meantime, since the Day of the Lord, when human power will be overthrown, is on the horizon: 'Then comes the end, when he hands over the kingdom to God the Father, after he has destroyed every ruler and every authority and power' (1 Cor. 15.24). The only viable system of government in biblical terms is a theocracy. Human kings and leaders can prosper in the sight of God, but only if they are directly adopted by the deity (1 Sam. 7) and God rules by extension.

The biblical narrative that runs through Judges and Ruth should not primarily be understood as offering good and bad variations of patriarchies, but rather variations of divine power paradigms that present a judgement on human power paradigms and ultimately demand the rejection of the latter. Various stages in the biblical narrative have been suggested for pinpointing the precise beginning in biblical narrative for the appointment of God's chosen one. Hints and allusions to the eventual fulfilment of divinely ordained governance in the person of King David are peppered throughout texts that precede the account in 2 Samuel. David's lineage is traced as far back as Tamar in Genesis 38 – a story we discussed in the previous chapter. A radical reading would anticipate the figure of David in the Eden narrative, where the ideal harmonious relationship between God and his 'first-born' is set out. The first couple's rejection of that ideal means that it remains unrealised and, in theological terms, it becomes a blueprint for a future redeemer figure. In Christian contexts this role is readily seized upon from earliest times as an archetype for Christ, and in Pauline theology Christ becomes the second Adam, succeeding where the first failed. Paul was able to take this theological step with apparent ease, as a Jew of the early first century CE who had been immersed in scripture and its interpretation all his life, thinking through the implications of a dying and rising messianic figure. In Christian contexts this theology has been reworked and developed down the centuries, from Augustine to Karl Barth. In the world of the biblical writers the expulsion from Eden explained the imperfections of human lives. But those imperfections inferred the possibility for perfection and the hope of a return to the ideal of oneness of will and purpose between God and his world, manifested through the rule of his anointed one. In this sense we can see the kernel of political theology that lies at the heart of the biblical agenda.

In the next chapter we will observe how divine omnipotence develops commensurately with the intensification and magnification of human power systems, and explore how the manipulation of gender becomes a more overt strategic tool in the elevation of the status of God.

5

CROSSING THE
BOUNDARIES

In the previous chapter we focused on texts that were produced during the Second Temple period in order to reflect on Israel's past in the light of a theology of a group that strove for a resurgence of national religion. The emergence of Hellenism as an imperial ideology further threatened the national identity and, with it, the religion of diminutive states in the ancient Near East. From the time of Alexander the Great, Israel would constantly struggle to maintain its distinctive identity amongst the waves of domination that flowed and ebbed over its borders and that challenged its diasporic communities. Over the next few centuries Ptolemies, Seleucids and, eventually, the Romans would all offer alternative paradigms of omnipotence. This period produced the sacred texts, or canons, of both emergent Judaism and Christianity.

In this chapter, as in the previous one, our focus will remain on the human characters whose actions and destinies reflect the power and constancy of the God of Israel. As we move into the world of ancient superpowers, however, it becomes more evident that those tensions become more clearly articulated in terms of the dangers of the 'outsiders' who would threaten the pre-eminence of that God. The book of Judith, together with some material from the Gospels of early Christianity, will be used to illustrate this development.

JUDITH

But the Lord Almighty has foiled them by the hand of a female ... Judith daughter of Merari with the beauty of her countenance undid him.

(Judith 16.5, 6b)

According to the book of Judith these are the words Judith sang at the thanksgiving after her slaughter of the nation's enemy, Holofernes. In this section we will try to uncover the gender games that are played out by male and female characters in order to reach the ultimate and bloody conclusion to the story.

Judith is an apocryphal text that unashamedly draws on numerous scenes and characters from the Hebrew Bible. The situation at the beginning of the narrative is dire; like the book of Ruth, the story begins with the air of hopelessness. In Ruth famine and death – the impossibility of regeneration – dominate the scene. In Judith the enemy's siege has created the same scene of hopeless despair. In both cases God is apparently passive, a shadowy figure lurking in the background, and in both cases it is female characters who take the initiative and transform the scene from one of death to life. But, as we noted in our discussion of Ruth, we should resist simply seizing on these narratives as protofeminist manifestos. Although van Henten (1995: 225, 245–52) refers to Craven (1983: 121) and van Dijk-Hemmes (Brenner and van Dijk-Hemmes 1993: 31), to warn against labelling a text that has a female main character as 'feminist', she does argue for partial female authorship for Judith on the basis of the representation of female characters, particularly Judith herself. We need to dig deeper to discover the theological agenda prompting the creation of these female characters and, what is more, to investigate the male characters and reflect on their role within the theocratic framework. These characters are being used to illustrate the anarchic chaos of a holy nation bereft of an active God. The author uses the device of unconventionality to subvert the readers' expectations, but his purpose is incidentally, and not ultimately, anarchic. The use of the female hero allows for God to act in the most unexpected fashion and to foil the enemies of his elect people through a female redeemer. Judith, like other biblical female heroic figures, is herself merely a literary device that serves the higher cause of God.

There is more to the book of Judith, however, than simply the surprise element of a female victor. To reach the intended goal, the character of Judith flows backwards and forwards across the gender spectrum, moving fluently from eyelash-fluttering feminine allure to sword-wielding masculine action. She evades concrete definition in either male or female category. Her speech and actions parody the given gender codes. Her 'masculinity' acts to ridicule her male contemporaries and, as woman, her femininity surpasses that of all other women. Some time ago Patricia Montley recognised the ambivalent nature of Judith's gender as it is depicted in the narrative. She remarks on the alternation of Judith between 'masculinity' and 'femininity' – between soldier and seductress – and comments that the character transcends the male and female dichotomy (1978: 40).

In allowing such fluidity in behaviour, we could ask further questions of the gender-play evident in the text. Does it subvert the very notion of the polarities of prescribed 'masculine' and 'feminine' behaviour? Does it forgo the gender essentialism that is so embedded in biblical societies? The text does answer these questions in the affirmative, and the greater the depth of gender subversion carried out by the author, the more the traditional modes of mere human behaviour patterns are ridiculed. Rather than an anarchic outcome, however, what eventually emerges is confirmation of the limitless power of the deity. The shadowy God lurking in the background of the narrative is the key operator – permitting and empowering the character of Judith to act beyond the given boundaries. Before we encounter the enigmatic Judith in the story we know that God has been petitioned to act:

> And all the Israelites, men, women and children living at Jerusalem prostrated themselves before the temple and put ashes on their heads and spread out their sackcloth before the Lord.
>
> (4.11)

Moreover, we are told that the Lord has heard their prayers and has regard for their distress (4.13), but this comment by the author functions as an aside to the audience and for the characters in the story their prayers remain unanswered. This same device is evident in the book of Job where the audience, unlike the main characters in the book, are given an insight into the heavenly court and know that Job's predicament is the result of a wager between God and Satan. As in the case of Job in the midst of his suffering, no remedy is in sight for the Israelites of the book of Judith.

In the story of Judith the fortified hill towns of Judea have become the focus for the enemy armies, led by Holofernes, and Bethulia, Judith's hometown, is being besieged. Exhausted and thirsty, the people of Bethulia are convinced that God has forsaken them and they prepare for surrender and inevitable slavery, choosing, while they still can, mere survival as opposed to total annihilation. One of their leaders, Uzziah, persuades them to give God five more days to intervene and save them.

The stage is now set for Judith's entrance into the narrative, and the ironic story of redemption by the hand of a female figure unfolds. We can justify emphasising the strength of the ironic element in the depiction of the figure of Judith when we look elsewhere in the text. André LaCocque points to the historical inaccuracies in the account and he considers them to be too numerous to be mere accident (1990: 31–48). Most notably, Nebuchadnezzar – who was, as we know, the Babylonian king who captured Jerusalem, destroyed the Temple, among other things, and instigated the Israelite exile in the sixth century BCE – becomes in the book of Judith the king of Assyria (1.1).

The names Holofernes and Bagoas (2.4; 12.11), although historical, are Persian and appear elsewhere participating in the campaign against Egypt under Artaxerxes III in 341 BCE. In Judith we are told that Judaea is led by Joakim the High Priest (4.6), a situation that occurred in 153 BCE in the time of Jonathan, brother of Judas Maccabee (1 Macc. 10.20). The time and the characters are deliberately and ironically fictitious, as is the place: the small Palestinian city of 'Bethulia', placed under siege, is unknown outside the book of Judith.

LaCocque is one amongst many scholars to focus on the irony evident in this text, and Moore comments that irony is 'the key to the book' (1985: 78). In his study of Judith, Luis Alonso-Schokel comments that, for irony to be effective, 'the "secret communion" or collusion of author and reader at the expense of some character is essential' (1975: 8). In Judith author and audience are fully aware of the fictitious nature of all these elements in the account – the audience enters into the 'game', willing participants in the ploy and expectant for the rest of the narrative to unfold and the purpose to be made manifest. The ridicule of the foreigner, the figure of Holofernes, is the most overt purpose – the one that provides immediate gratification at his beheading. The narrative provides ample entertainment by giving Holofernes plenty of dialogue that resounds with double entendres, ridiculing his vanity and masculinity. This purpose, localised in the story's characters, coexists with the overriding intent to glorify God.

A scene of helplessness – with the people of Bethulia prepared to surrender to the enemy rather than face death – prompts the entrance of Judith into the narrative. The extended opening section of seven chapters builds up an atmosphere of anticipation and, with the introduction of 'fake' characters and places and the rewriting of past events, the audience is ready and waiting for the challenge of the unexpected. This mood of expectation contrived by the author is typical in biblical narrative. A cyclical pattern of redemption, where God's people sin, are punished, call on God for help, and are then redeemed through a divinely inspired new leader, is evident throughout Joshua, Judges and the books of Kings. In Judges 4 we find another example of God answering the people's distress with a female figure, Deborah, whose intervention, with that of Jael in the same narrative, has been identified as the inspiration for Judith's role by many commentators (White 1992: 5–16).

What is striking about Judith's first appearance in the narrative is that she is introduced with her own genealogy, that is, using the convention that is usually preserved for men (8.1). Immediately the biblical gender boundaries, consistently reinforced by conventions such as this, are made unstable. This is our first marker for 'discontinuity'. Furthermore, this lineage is not traced through her husband, but through her own male relatives, and is taken back as far as her forefather, Israel. Her husband, Manasseh, we are told, died of heatstroke during a barley harvest. Levine (1995: 212–13) understands the description of Judith's husband's death as a prefiguring of Holofernes' decapitation. Manasseh's death, coupled with the unpleasant associations of the name he shares with the King of Judah whose rule culminated in the devastating Babylonian invasion, provides the reader with sufficient information to conclude that Judith's subsequent heroic actions are clearly not in line with her husband's history. By tracing her genealogy apart from her husband's, Judith's identity is made distinct from him.

Judith appears as an autonomous individual who has selected her own way of life. The only link maintained with her identity as wife of Manasseh is the wealth she inherited from him. But the inheritance gives her the means of autonomy – this wealth enables her to be independent of men. No mention is made of any pressure on her to remarry or, in the context of Israelite society, to undergo a levirate marriage – an option adapted in the case of Tamar and Ruth (see Chapters 3 and 4, this volume). The text remains silent on this question.

As a wealthy widow Judith is manoeuvred into a position outside the prescribed gender roles of her society. The notion of relatively independent wealthy widows is not unknown in other contemporary contexts in the ancient world. In Roman society during the second century BCE the huge losses suffered during the military campaigns of the Punic wars led to a significant increase in the number of women who inherited wealth as a result of the deaths of fathers, husbands and brothers. The concerns regarding this situation led in 215 BCE to the *lex oppia* legislation being passed by Senate (Sawyer 1996: 22–3). This law explicitly restricted the ways in which women could use their wealth. They were forbidden to own more than half an ounce of gold, to wear robes trimmed with purple, or to ride about Rome in carriages drawn by two horses. This law was in force for twenty years before it was met with explicit opposition and returned to Senate for repeal. During the debate Livy recounts how women protested in the streets outside the Senate building. One of the speeches, by a known reactionary of the day, Cato the Elder, in favour of maintaining the law aptly encapsulates the recognised threat to society posed by women of independent means:

> What they want is complete freedom – or, not to mince words, complete licence. If they carry this present issue by storm, what will they not try next? Just consider the number of regulations imposed in the past to restrain their licence and subject them to their husbands. Even with these in force, you can still hardly control them. Suppose you allow them to acquire or extort one right after another, and in the end to achieve complete equality with men, do you think you will find them bearable? Nonsense. Once they have achieved equality, they will be your masters.
>
> (Livy 34.2–4, cited in Balsdon 1962: 34)

Closer to the world-view of the writer of Judith, this concept of wealthy, independent women was not unknown in early Jewish society. Judith Wegner has demonstrated that, in mishnaic times, widows achieved levels of autonomy comparable to their pagan neighbours within the Roman Empire. Obviously, we have to be careful in using this evidence to draw conclusions about a society that predates the mishnaic era. But Wegner's comment that the mishnaic sages seemed to perceive the autonomous widow's thought processes as similar to those of a man does help to illustrate how the character of Judith might have been perceived in terms of one standing outside conventional expectations for women (1988: 143).

When we set Judith's situation in the wider context of the ancient world, we can see more clearly the distinctive nature of her independence, and the challenge it could pose to traditional restrictions on women's lives. As a wealthy widow Judith does not have to seek out male support. She needs neither the material support of a man, nor a male partner to provide her with a child. To be presented with a central female figure in the biblical tradition who is childless and, moreover, is not seeking for this predicament to be remedied, either by divine or human intervention, is an interesting feature. As we have seen, the role Judith is destined to play is certainly not connected to her husband in any way, and neither is it connected to her offspring. Although we find allusions in the narrative to women such as Sarah, Rebekah, Rachel, Tamar, Naomi and Ruth, all these women were active or defined in relation to procreation, or to ensuring that the interests of their favoured child were met. Judith's apparent childlessness, together with the indifference of the text on this matter, places our character outside the category of these women. In this context the only comparable female biblical figures are Deborah and Jael. The text is silent in regard to their offspring and, although Deborah is described as 'a mother in Israel' (Judg. 5.7), this description, for once, is not related to actual motherhood, but to her charge of God's people.

Judith, then, is allowed to remain her 'own person', independent of husband and children, and her wealth enables this unusual situation to be sustained. Rather than flaunt this wealth, a criticism often levelled at the rich women of the Roman world, Judith chooses to lead an exceptionally pious life. This, again, marks her out as unconventional. Judith's piety is not prompted by any obvious need for which she might petition her God. She is not destitute. Although without husband or children, she is not seeking for this situation to be changed. She lives a life of prayer and holiness simply because she is religious. This faith provides her with theological insight and allows her to admonish her own people for daring to put God to the test. Her faith prompts her to take the risk of entering the enemy's camp. Judith embodies all the attributes of the Maccabean martyrs of the author's own day, who resisted the might of Antiochus IV and sacrificed their lives rather than deny their faith and identity. Ironically, in this narrative Judith's self-sacrifice stops short of martyrdom and this holy innocent becomes the bloody executioner. Judith's identity as a holy person enables her character to explode the given gender categories and act on God's behalf as the ruthless soldier of divine retribution. This feature is another marker of 'discontinuity'. This radical piety takes Judith outside either male or female categories.

In her admonishment of her people who would dare to question the ways of God and, moreover, to test God's love for Israel, Judith's first direct speech echoes the theology of the book of Job, or rather the theology voiced by God 'himself' in Job 38. The comparison with Job is noted by Linda Bennett Elder (1995: 449). We should note that in the case of Job it is God himself who voices this theology (Job 38), whereas here it comes from the lips of a woman. The God of Israel, she tells them, is not restricted to behave in given patterns, 'for God is not like a human being, to be threatened, or like a mere mortal to be won over with pleading' (8.16). God is beyond human reasoning, so we can expect divine action to burst out of the bounds that limit human possibilities. Judith personifies such suprahuman possibilities in her mercurial gender transitions.

She uses the argument of God, related in the book of Job, to admonish her people. In other words, she speaks as God – she makes known the mind of God. This insight into the divine mind, or this unique alliance with God, is evident in the unwavering confidence she has in her actions. In the prayer she makes before embarking on her visit to Holofernes, she does not ask God to show her what to do, she only asks for divine strength to fulfil her plan. She knows her plan is the right one, despite its ingredients of deceit and murder. God becomes the accessory to the act, not the originator of it, nor the prime mover: 'Make *my* deceitful words bring wound and bruise' (9.13). There are, of course, many biblical examples of women who deceive with God's blessing and, for example, in the case of Rebekah, with God as the author of the deception (Gen. 25.23; 27). Tamar's deception of Judah (Gen. 38), although not a direct divine command, does form an integral part of God's plan for the nation of Israel.

As we have noted, many scholars have observed the apparent parallel between Judith and Jael – both women commit an act of murder on behalf of the people, and both carry out this act by deceiving the victim through a sense of false security. Judith tricks Holofernes into believing that there will be a night of lovemaking in his tent, while Jael led Sisera to her tent with the expectation that he would receive respite and sustenance. This process of deception is vital since both women are physically weaker than their respective prey. A key difference between these two accounts is that, in the case of Sisera's murder, the author provides no insight into the mind of Jael. In the case of Judith's story, however, we are told explicitly that she has planned the deception – the murder is premeditated (9.9–10). So the act is a deliberate one, and Judith the definitive protagonist.

As the narrative moves towards its climax, Judith strides across the gender spectrum and transforms from a figure who, as the autonomous pious widow, has so far defied categorisation in the binary gender construction, but who now arrives at the extreme polarity of femininity. Ironically, it is in this guise that she will redeem Israel. The author stresses this switch of identity. Judith is not allowed merely to drift from 'non-feminine' to feminine – she consciously 'becomes' feminine. Her change of dress code, change of demeanour and change of language achieve this transformation. She crosses over to the world of sexual activity and wears the signals of availability:

> She removed the sackcloth she had been wearing, took off her widow's garments, bathed her body with water, and anointed herself with precious ointment. She combed her hair, put on a tiara, and dressed herself in the festive attire she used to wear while her husband Manasseh was living. She put sandals on her feet, and put on her anklets, bracelets, rings, earrings, and all her other jewellery. Thus she made herself very beautiful, to entice the eyes of all the men who might see her.
>
> (10.3–4)

Prior to this pivotal moment in the narrative, Judith's singularity has been characterised by her autonomy – her lack of dependence on husband or family, her independent wealth and her chosen piety. This autonomy has empowered her to speak with authority to her male 'superiors' and to be heard by them. Yet this guise is set aside for the task of vanquishing the enemy. For this she assumes the familiar guise of seductress, guaranteed to succeed since the time of Eve. A work contemporary with the book of Judith leaves us in no doubt as to this dangerous guise of womankind: 'Do not be ensnared by a woman's beauty. . . . From a woman sin had its beginning, and because of her we all die' (Ecclus. 25.21, 24). It would have served Holofernes well to have taken counsel on the female 'other' from Jesus Ben Sirach.

Although, when the time of the fatal deed arrives, Holofernes has inadvertently made his own murder a somewhat easy task by getting himself dead drunk, the author still uses this moment to switch Judith's guise again and allows the readers to renew their acquaintance with the autonomous Judith. In her speech immediately prior to taking up the sword, she does not ask God for strength, but for God to witness the act:

> O Lord God of all might, look in this hour on the work of
> my hands for the exaltation of Jerusalem. Now indeed is
> the time to help your heritage and to carry out *my design* to
> destroy the enemies who have risen up against us.
>
> (13.4–5)

One obvious biblical doublet to this scene is David's victory over
Goliath. It can be argued that Judith's act is of a weaker order than
that of David – as would be appropriate since Judith is a woman.
First, unlike Goliath, Holofernes is drunk and unconscious, and,
second, it takes Judith two strikes of the sword to decapitate her
victim, whereas David achieved it with one stroke. However, in both
stories there are three stages to the beheading. David first immo-
bilises Goliath by aiming a stone at his head, then he kills him, and
after he is dead he cuts off the head. In Judith, Holofernes is immo-
bilised – by drink – then there are two strokes of the sword to kill
him and to decapitate him. Both David and Judith fall outside the
category of male warriors: Judith because she is female, and David
because he is not yet an adult male – he is 'just a boy' (1 Sam. 17.33).
Both characters step outside the normal behavioural expectations
through their actions. The author of the account of David and Goliath
and the author of Judith utilise the physically implausible as a literary device to subvert the readers' expectations, and in both cases the
ultimate purpose is to point to the unfathomable ways of God.

On her triumphant return to her city, Judith displays her booty
of Holofernes' head to the crowd. Here the gender card is played in
a finesse: 'The Lord has struck him down by the hand of a female.
. . . I swear that it was my face that seduced him to his destruction'
(13.15–16). Traditional male territory has been trespassed by a
female – boundaries have been challenged and dislodged.

The enemy of Israel has suffered the ultimate humiliation. Judith,
as a femme fatale, has succeeded in her plan. What we should
remember is that she translated herself into this guise. Like Tamar,
she moved out of the mode of non-sexual widow to that of seductress in order to secure her goal. Unlike Tamar, Judith was powerful
and assertive in her widowed state and, unlike Tamar, her goal was
more overtly political. Judith's widowhood was of a different order
to that of Tamar. She was rich and politically involved, with a direct
line to God. Tamar was without identity – destitute and powerless
– and her body was her only instrument for survival. Unlike Judith,
she had to perform the sexual act to succeed – Judith remained
'undefiled'.

The guise of seductress is quickly removed from Judith. We are told that she loads up her mules with Holofernes' silverware and furniture. Again she has crossed over the gender spectrum and her behaviour is that of a triumphant male warrior at the victorious close of battle. Judith and the women of Israel then enjoy a celebration of the victory. Although this scene can be read as Judith returning to where she belongs – alongside the women – alternative readings are possible. One parallel brought to mind by this scene is, again, the episode with David and Goliath. When David and Saul returned victorious from the battle with the Philistines, the women came out from all the towns of Israel singing and dancing (1 Sam. 18.6–9). Their words in praise of David become a taunt to Saul – just as the triumph of Judith stands as an emasculation of the men of Israel who had been ineffective against Holofernes. The victories of both Judith and David unsettle the males in the narrative and the intention of both authors is no doubt to unsettle their essentially male audience, the purpose being to point out the unpredictable nature of divine intervention. The chorus of women recognise the achievement of the unconventional warrior, and we are able to observe how gender games have been employed to subvert the expected, embedded norms of this ancient socio-political context.

Although by the end of the narrative Judith had retreated from the centre stage of Israelite politics, she remained active and assertive. She did not marry and have children. She lived as a wealthy widow whose fame, we are told, grew and grew. At the end of her life, at the great age of 105, she distributed her property herself, to both her own and her former husband's family, and she set her maid free. She remained the autonomous figure.

In the book of Judith the explosion of possibilities acted out on a female body and the subsequent divine victory wrought through this form is contrasted sharply by the emasculation of the book's male characters. The function of the eunuch Bagoas – Holofernes' personal attendant – has been understood in psychoanalytical terms. His lack of genitalia mirrors the symbolic castration of his master and the story is understood to articulate the primitive subconscious male fear of castration, while Achior's circumcision, or his symbolic castration, is, in Margarita Stocker's words 'a formal submission to God: as it were, an acknowledgement of the greater virility or power exercised by the ultimate patriarch' (1998: 7). She continues:

> The most striking element in the Book of Judith is that it is so conscious and deliberate in its acknowledgement of the

phallic concept of power. If power is patriarchal, then the
only possessor of supreme masculinity is God.

(1998: 7)

God, then, stands centre stage as the true Freudian 'big daddy' and,
as such, his sons struggle to be 'real' men – always destined to be
overshadowed and incomplete.

Holofernes, Achior and Bagoas are all emasculated in various ways;
likewise, the men of Israel with their male leaders are presented as
feeble passive recipients of their fate. Achior is a relatively useful
male character – but, as a foreigner, despite his recent circumcision, and as more of an observer than an instigator, he remains
on the sidelines. The female characters, Judith, her attendant-cum-
accomplice and the women who greet and affirm her on her victorious return, are the only truly worthy supporters for this macho
divinity. Judith embodied in female form – despite her various
performances – presents a safe counterpart to the male God. She can
be elevated without any risk of phallus rivalry. She allows the God
of Israel to be *the* superpower in a world where larger-than-life
emperors offer alternative, and even divine, paradigms to Israel's God
(see Chapter 6, this volume).

Judith's actions in the narrative demonstrate how gender-games
could be utilised by an ancient writer to produce his desired purpose.
By creating a character that represented a counter-culture, and by
moving the figure across the gender spectrum, the power of the deity
is made absolute. The conceptualisation of gender as performance is
not a new discovery made by late-twentieth-century postmodern
theorists. It is evident in the ancient world. We find it in the book
of Judith, and it is also evident in the Graeco-Roman world, a good
example being the *galli* priests of the Magna Mater cult (Beard 1994:
168–9). These 'male' priests castrated themselves and dressed in
women's clothes. Yet they were sexually active with women. They
defied the gender codes of their own day, a period contemporary
with the author of Judith, and attracted the disapproval of the
conventional minds of their time. In Judith the gender-games are
more tentative, but serve as a powerful literary device.

Of course such gender-play is allowed for God in the biblical
narrative. Feminist theologians have brought to the fore texts that
show God, who is always given the masculine pronoun by the
biblical writers, displaying behaviour that is normally reserved for
females. Indeed, Deuteronomy 32.18 even allows 'him' to give birth.
Examples such as this underline divine uniqueness that surpasses

human gender constraints. Judith is an important and, perhaps unique, example of a character who, like God, is allowed to break these constraints and stride across the gender spectrum.

The ideas of gender theorists, in particular Irigaray and Butler, allow us to interrogate the figure of Judith in more fluid terms, liberating us from defining the character at the polarities of a given binary gender construction. Informed by the insights of Irigaray's understanding of a new essentialism, we can see Judith as a figure who, as encountered and perceived by Holofernes, enacts what woman might be expected to be, but, as a *mimesis* of that category, she parodies and subverts the given boundaries. A new and unique 'woman' emerges from and through her experience. Such a woman stands in stark contrast to the unnamed butchered woman described in Judges 19 (see Chapter 4, this volume). The beheading of Holofernes is depicted in all its bloody violence by the Renaissance artist Artemisia Gentileschi (1593–*c*. 1651), who perfected the pose of Judith by practising dismemberment on a pig's carcass. Margarita Stocker comments on the representation in the painting of Holofernes' arms, which are stretched out like a woman's parted thighs. Holofernes' powerlessness in the face of this violence perhaps mirrors Gentileschi's own experience of rape (*Judith and Holofernes*, Galleria degli Uffizi, Florence; Stocker 1998: 17; see also Greer 1981: 189–207). In this reading Judith's act can be seen as the ultimate revenge for male brutality against women, and the parody of the female other.

Alternatively, working with Butler's model of deconstruction, we might understand Judith as an individual figure who performs gender across a spectrum of possibilities, defying clear identification within any given constructed role. Whatever the author's theological intention might have been, the elusive figure of Judith offers us a subversive, even anarchic, paradigm of gender-play evident within the theocratic metanarrative of biblical tradition.

GOSPEL TRADITIONS

The shift within this chapter from the book of Judith, set as it is in the context of Israelite religion at the time of the emergence of synagogue faith and early Judaism, to the context of early Christianity may seem abrupt. The book of Judith, however, has been understood by Elisabeth Schüssler Fiorenza as a text that does convincingly contextualise the world of the first-century Jesus movement (1995b:

115–18). In her representation of Christian origins Fiorenza accepts the criticism of Jewish feminist writers who have exposed contemporary Christian feminist theologians to be anti-Jewish in their identification of any 'anti-woman' comment in early Christian literature with that new religion's Jewish heritage (Plaskow 1978; 1993). In doing so, Fiorenza takes the book of Judith to illustrate that, although patriarchy was dominant in Judaism, as it was throughout the ancient world, there was diversity within the tradition that allowed for the possibility of female agency. In the light of the story of Judith: 'It seems greatly misleading, therefore, to picture Jewish women of the first century in particular, and Jewish theology generally, in predominantly negative terms' (1995b: 118). While Fiorenza uses the characterisation of Judith to contextualise the gender-inclusive teaching within certain strands of early Christianity, she does tend to dilute the action of that character through a spiritualisation of her actions: 'Intelligent wisdom, observant piety, shrewd observation, and faithful dedication to the liberation of her people are Judith's true definition and personal assets' (1995b: 117). Fiorenza's further comment that 'wisdom prevailed over brute power' (1995b: 118) is in stark contrast to interpretations that do accommodate the true violence of Judith's act, such as the paintings of Artemisia Gentileschi. In Fiorenza's reading of Judith we can see the apologetic nature of feminist theology at work – trapped between delving into texts to find images that affirm female agency and resisting the application of a stringent hermeneutics of suspicion to the character of the biblical God. Fiorenza does not dwell on the question of the nature of a God who would empower a woman to hack off a man's head, but instead blurs the issue by seeing it all as an act of liberation of the oppressed through divine intervention.

Although a 'fringe' text in canonical terms, the book of Judith does reveal that there are paradigms for 'being woman' that diverge from the given norms for female status and behaviour outlined in the biblical legislative and didactic literature. Furthermore, these divergent paradigms are not included to further some protofeminist agenda of the ancient world, but rather to illustrate the nature of the biblical God – to show how divine activity is utterly unrestricted by human norms. This theme was particularly valuable to emerging Christianity, and was readily taken up and utilised by the new religion's early writers. The Jesus movement in the first decades after the events of the founder's death, had to present a belief that stretched human credulity to its limits: 'For Jews demand signs and Greeks desire wisdom, but we proclaim Christ crucified, a stumbling block to Jews and foolishness to Gentiles' (1 Cor. 1.22). Here Paul of Tarsus neatly presents the paradox at the heart of the earliest theology that emerged from this Jewish messianic movement. The Messiah (termed χριστος in Paul's diaspora Greek) had appeared, but, instead of leading God's glorious and victorious armies against Israel's alien occupying force, he had been executed in the manner of a common criminal. The conviction held by the early followers that Jesus of Nazareth had been raised from the dead by the hand of God fired their missionary zeal and prompted a theology that dared to comes to terms with such a strange notion of messiahship. Paul also periodises the messianic age after the fashion of apocalyptic eschatology in order to make sense of the impossibility of a crucified messiah:

> For as all die in Adam, so all will be made alive in Christ. But each in his own order: Christ the first fruits, then at his coming those who belong to Christ. Then comes the end, when he hands over the kingdom to God the Father, after he has destroyed every ruler and every authority and power.
>
> (1 Cor. 15.22–4)

The Messiah in the form of Jesus of Nazareth has only begun his messianic mission. Having been raised in glory he now sits at God's right hand awaiting the next stage in the divine redemption plan when a more recognisable messianic victory will be made manifest. In biblical tradition, Paul the Jew, writing in the first half of the first century, uses the theme of the anarchic God to underpin the radical theology he is formulating: 'For God's foolishness is wiser than human wisdom, and God's weakness is stronger than human strength' (1 Cor. 1.25). God cannot be 'read' according to human measures. This line of argument pursued by Paul echoes the theology of the book of Job, where God responds to Job's impertinent questioning of theodicy with the unanswerable line, 'Where were you when I laid the foundation of the earth?' (Job 38.4; see Chapter 2, this volume).

In the light of unique divine omnipotence and omniscience the only viable human response is to worship and obey. Paul expresses the revelation of Jesus as the awaited messiah in similar vein. We cannot fathom the workings of the divine plan for the redemption of God's creation and his elect. In fact, the more implausible the evidence, the more likely it is that divine wisdom is at work, for, as just mentioned, 'God's foolishness is wiser than human wisdom, and God's weakness is stronger than human strength' (1 Cor. 1.25).

Not only do early articulators within the Jesus movement draw on biblical speculative literature as a source of proof-texts for their emerging beliefs, they also take up the biblical theme of gender-play as a tool for displaying the incongruities between human expectation and divine schemes.

Among the early Christian texts, canonical and non-canonical, there is a variety of notions of gender and sexual hierarchy to be found in the descriptions of the ministry of Jesus and the early faith communities. Such divergence testifies to the plurality within early Christianity, or rather to the pluralism among early christianities and their emergent theologies. The Gospel writers do share a consistency, however, in terms of their use of gender as a literary strategy, and this can be observed from the roles they give to certain female and male disciples in their narratives. It is apparent particularly in relation to the use of female characters in the Gospels of Mark and John.

Fiorenza picks out these two canonical texts to illustrate 'a very different ethos of Christian discipleship and community than that presented by the writers of the injunctions to patriarchal submissions' (1995b: 316). Mary Rose D'Angelo also pairs these Gospels to interrogate them in terms of their presentations of women (1999). The writers who produced these two Gospels each develop a contrast within their narratives between female and male discipleship in order to illustrate a 'right' and 'wrong' way to be a true believer.

The purpose of discussing this material here is not to ascertain the precise role of women within the Jesus movement – a misguided and impossible task – but rather to ask why the evangelists selected particular traditions about women disciples and how they achieved their purpose via these characters within their narratives. As D'Angelo comments, the key task should be 'to trace out the ways that women and gender function in the literary and theological enterprises of the texts' (1999: 130). Feminist biblical scholars have tended to use the evidence in the Gospels and other early writings as a starting point to uncover Jesus' teaching about women and his understanding of their status within his ministry and, ultimately, within the Kingdom of God. The past then validates present-day calls for radical theological and ecclesiastical reform.

The existence within these ancient texts of stories about particular women can be taken as evidence of a 'depatriarchalised' strand within biblical literature that bears witness to a belief system that surpasses particular patriarchal societies. Indeed, Elisabeth Gössmann identifies what she terms a women's 'counter-tradition' that can be traced not only in biblical texts, but through patristic, medieval and Enlightenment literature, and is consistent up to and including the feminist theologians in our own time (1999). While there is no doubt that such evidence exists, and that figures from the past have encouraged and prompted successive generations of women, today's feminists need to be realistic about why these figures were carved into history – particularly those that are the product of a particular type of theology that was directed at an essentially male audience. This theology is not an unconscious revelation of a 'depatriarchalised' strand within tradition, but rather a conscious use of gender as a destabilising literary strategy. Antoinette Wire argues for a similar stance in relation to deciphering the role of female characters in Matthew's Gospel. By exemplifying ideal faith, women and other marginal characters teach the male audience about true discipleship – ironically, the illiterate train the literate (1991). Female characters in the Gospels – particularly those depicted in the Gospels of Mark and John – can shine out as ideal disciples, not necessarily because they are based on significant historical figures, but rather because the type of submission embodied in traditional female behaviour is more preferable in the sight of God than male autonomy. As we have noted in previous chapters, the submission that stems from total dependency as exemplified in the child/parent relationship is even more desirable, and we will discuss this in relation to early Christianity in the next chapter.

Before we examine the strategic use of female figures in Mark's Gospel, we should note that we find also in this Gospel, almost as a sub-plot, the story of John the Baptist's beheading – an event that is instigated by two female characters: Herodias, the wife of Herod Antipas, and her daughter (6.14–29). The author presents us, through these two women, with characters that are in line with other wicked women in biblical tradition, including Potophar's wife, Jezebel, and Delilah. All of these women possess a female tendency evident since their mother, Eve, to subvert or trick male characters – a trait paradoxically shared by the 'good' women, who are revered rather than damned because their trickery is in the service of God. Herod is duped and 'deeply grieved' (6.26) (περίλυπος – the same adjective used by the author of Mark to describe Jesus' state of mind in Gethsemane; see p. 105). Herod has given his word to grant whatever his daughter requests and, in doing so, innocently falls into the women's trap. However reluctantly, Herod has to order the beheading. This example of female scheming is not in the service of God, and the prophet, a 'righteous and holy man' (6.20) who was chosen to herald the arrival of God's Messiah, is slaughtered. This interlude in the Gospel presents an ironic reversal to the climax of the book of Judith, where a man is also beheaded through the intent of two women, but in that instance the act is in collusion with, rather than in opposition to, the deity.

In Mark's Gospel female figures are used strategically to symbolise the radical inclusive character of the Kingdom that Jesus' mission inaugurates. As women they already symbolise one level of exclusion within a patriarchal society, and the author of the Gospel underscores this by including accounts of Jesus encountering women who are further marginalised by their uncleanness (5.25–34), foreignness (7.24–30) and poverty (12.41–4). In Mark's Gospel the faith of women such as these is presented as exemplary, and often contrasted to the male disciples, even those closest to Jesus, who consistently fall short of this ideal. Perhaps the clearest picture of this type of contrast emerges towards the conclusion of the Gospel. The first example is the account of the woman who anoints Jesus at Bethany, and this scene opens the events that lead up to the passion narrative. The narrator has informed his readers that 'The chief priests and the scribes were looking for a way to arrest Jesus by stealth and kill him' (14.1), and this is followed by the anointing scene that vividly anticipates Jesus' death. The woman is unnamed and, together with the account given of her actions, this suggests similarities in terms of literary strategy to the account of the Samaritan woman in John's Gospel (see pp. 107–12). Both anonymous women are set in contrast to the male companions of Jesus in terms of their faith and their willingness to translate that faith into action.

In contemporary feminist biblical scholarship the woman who anoints Jesus has become the icon of the forgotten discipleship of women. Fiorenza takes this story as the centrepiece of her reconstruction of Christian origins and uses Jesus' words to this woman, as recorded in Mark's Gospel, as the title of her work, 'in memory of her' (Mark 14.9; Fiorenza 1995b). Fiorenza tells us that 'the name of the faithful disciple is forgotten because she was a woman' (1995b: xliii). However, non-naming can be a more effective device than naming in certain contexts (see the discussion of Judges 19 in Chapter 4) and certainly stresses the contrast between the named male disciples and the anonymous women whose active faith is undistracted by personal identity. The point is not that the author of Mark 'lost' this woman's name, but that he did not name her

deliberately. Namelessness signals a total lack of self – a key require-
ment for the children of God (Gal. 3.28). This woman is presented
as a prophetic figure who has understood and accepted the true
nature of Jesus' messiahship. Just as Samuel anointed the kings Saul
and David (1 Sam. 9.27–10.1, 16.1–13), this woman anoints Jesus'
head, taking on the role of prophet/priest and performing the rite
that confirms kingship (D'Angelo 1999: 143). But Jesus' kingship
is distinct from that of his ancestors. His reign will culminate in
crucifixion, offering the world the true icon of royal service (Mark
10.45, 15.39). The woman understands this, accepts it and has faith
in this type of messiahship. In contrast, the disciples consistently
reject or misunderstand the nature of Jesus' mission when it is
revealed to them (8.31–3, 9.30–2, 10.32–45; Martin (1972)
summarises the main theories that scholars have put forward during
the first half of the twentieth century to explain such themes in
Marcan theology). This woman's action is met with derision by the
assembled group at the house in Bethany. They are horrified that
money has been wasted to purchase such expensive ointment. Only
Jesus recognises the significance of the act and pronounces that this
woman, through her action of faith, will be remembered. The author
of Mark does not say that she will be remembered, but that what
she has done will stand in remembrance. Her action is a paradigm
of faith for the community the author is addressing and that is why
her name is unimportant. Immediately after the anointing scene we
are presented with a deliberate act in sharp contrast to that of the
woman. She has spent money to honour Jesus in the most appropriate manner, but then we are told of a named disciple, Judas, who
has plotted to betray Jesus in order to gain financial reward
(14.10–11; Tolbert 1992: 271).

The Gospel continues with its account of Jesus' last days before
his death, and the contrast intensifies between the type of discipleship evident in the actions of women and that displayed by the male
disciples. The scene at Gethsemane begins with an intimate account
of Jesus with his closest disciples, Peter, James and John, where
Jesus, echoing the words of the Psalmist, faces up to the horrific fate
that awaits him: 'My soul is deeply grieved' (περιλυπος εστιν η
ψυχη μου (14.34; see also Ps. 43.5)). Despite the desperate situation and Jesus' obvious distress, these chosen few doze off to sleep,
unresponsive to their master's repeated pleas to remain awake. The
scene moves on to the moment of Jesus' arrest, instigated by Judas'
kiss of betrayal, and the latter's identity as a chosen disciple is underlined: 'one of the twelve' (εις των δωδεκα) (14.43).

Between Jesus' trial before the Sanhedrin and his appearance before the Roman governor Pilate, the author places an episode that encapsulates the polemic against the male disciples that has been gradually intensifying through the second part of the narrative. In this scene Peter is confronted by one of the high priest's servant girls (των παιδισκων του αρχιεπεως) (14.66) and she identifies him as one of Jesus' followers. Peter immediately denies this and she challenges him twice more, but each time Peter refuses to admit to being a follower of Jesus. This three-fold denial had already been prophesied to him by Jesus during the Passover meal that Jesus had celebrated with the twelve (14.17ff.), although Peter had protested, 'Even though I must die with you, I will not deny you.' Also we are told, 'And all of them said the same' (14.31). Ironically, the only act of integrity that is executed during Jesus' final days is the woman's anointing. In contrast the male disciples fail miserably: Judas betrays him (14.43–4), all of them desert Jesus and flee from him (14.50) and Peter repeatedly denies he ever knew him (14.66–72). Women are placed strategically within this climactic part of the narrative to highlight the shortcomings of the twelve and, at the same time, to offer paradigms for true discipleship.

Jesus' crucifixion and death is portrayed in Mark as a ghastly and lonely scene, epitomised in Jesus' cry, given in his mother tongue, 'Eloi, Eloi, lema sabachthani?', which means 'My God, my God, why have you forsaken me?' This depiction of human agony contrasts with the account given by the author of Luke's Gospel, who pictures a crucifixion without pain and with Jesus ministering to those who are being crucified beside him. In Mark's account Jesus is surrounded by hostile strangers. At the moment of his death, one of these strangers, a centurion, suddenly grasps the significance of the event (15.39), but the chosen twelve are not even present. The only sign of consolation in this scene of lonely desolation is the appearance of the women who had been a constant presence in Jesus' ministry. We are told that they were 'looking on from a distance' (15.40), signalling that they too were in danger, but that they were willing to take a calculated risk in order to minister to Jesus at his death. These events prompt Fiorenza to comment, 'The women are thus characterized as true disciples of Jesus who have left everything and have followed him on the way, even to its bitter end on the cross' (1995b: 320).

Ultimately, in Mark the female disciples remain paradigms for faith rather than 'real' characters that could form the foundation of an apostolic tradition parallel to their male counterparts. Even though the male disciples fail Jesus, it is these twelve he hand-picked and called by name. They are the human side of discipleship, revealing the true difficulties of remaining constant in their faith – a dilemma strikingly apposite for the Gospel's intended readership, who themselves face the dreadful persecutions of Emperor Nero. The women in the Gospel function simply, but effectively, as a literary strategy to stir up the (male) audience – a point succinctly expressed by Joanna Dewey:

> But Mark's Gospel remains an androcentric narrative. Mark uses these stories not so much to empower women to be followers of Jesus in their own right, as for didactic purposes. He uses women to encourage his audience, perhaps especially the men in his audience, to follow a discipleship of service. Mark may even be using the women to shame the men into doing better.
>
> (1995: 508)

A similar strategy in regard to female figures can be identified in John's Gospel. The story of the Samaritan woman in that Gospel is a critical text for the present study since it comprises the longest piece of dialogue with Jesus recorded in a canonical Gospel, and, moreover, deliberately highlights the question of gender through the inclusion of this aside by the writer:

> Just then the disciples came. They were astonished that he was speaking with a woman, but no one said, 'What do you want?' or, 'Why are you speaking with her?'
>
> (John 4.27)

As many scholars, including Mary Margaret Pazdan (1987), Gail O'Day (1992) and Raymond Collins (1995), have pointed out, the Samaritan woman portrayed in the Gospel stands in stark contrast to the figure of Nicodemus – another individual, presented in the previous chapter, who had a theological dialogue with Jesus. Nicodemus is described as a Pharisee and αρχων των Ἰουδαιων (3.1) – a pillar of the Jerusalem Jewish community. The Samaritan woman is unnamed, a foreigner in relation to Jesus and his disciples, and living on the fringes of her own society. But it is through the story of this woman that the author of John's Gospel presents us with one of the most engaging conversations recorded in the Bible, certainly in relation to the person of Jesus. As Adele Reinhartz comments, this encounter, along with the account of the two sisters, Mary and Martha (11.1–44), 'marks one of the few occasions in this Gospel in which a dialogue between Jesus and another character does not become a monologue for Jesus alone' (1995: 573). The exchange with the Samaritan woman includes insight, argument and humour, and, above all, mutual respect.

Jesus and the woman meet at Jacob's well, situated in the Samaritan town Sychar (known as Shechem in the Hebrew Bible), and the possibility for symbolic interpretations of this setting has attracted many theories from commentators. For example, it is possible to find here a deliberate allusion to Moses' flight from Egypt and his encounter with the Midianites (Exod. 2.15–22) – both figures flee from persecution and seek hospitality in a foreign land. Lyle Eslinger argues that this setting prompts the reader to identify the scene as one of betrothal in the light of Moses' experience in Exodus 2 (1987: 174), and it is also reminiscent of the meetings between Isaac and Rebecca (Gen. 24) and Jacob and Rachel (Gen. 29.1–20) (Streete 1997: 144). In her recent study of gender characterisation in John's Gospel, Colleen Conway offers a critical and convincing assessment of these symbolic interpretations. She concludes that there is significant nuptual imagery evident in the wider context of the story (2.1–11; 3.29), and this, together with the actual setting, prompts her to conclude that 'gender is not coincidental to the story, but a major component of the narrative' (1999: 109).

There is certainly a ready rapport between Jesus and this woman – sufficient to cause his disciples concern that Jesus might be compromising his reputation (4.27). Similarly, for past generations of scholars this woman has posed a threat to the status quo of traditional religion. First, although innocuous to many present-day readers, her presence and the lively exchange she enjoys with Jesus have raised the issue of Jesus' relations with women – or, even more uncomfortably, his sexuality. Second, in a tradition that has preferred women to remain silent on the subject of theology, this woman is singled out by Jesus to participate in the longest theological dialogue in the Gospels. Generations of commentators have dealt with this encounter by putting the woman into categories that remove her from such dangerous territory. O'Day neatly sums up the history of this character's treatment by traditional scholarship:

> First, many commentators raise questions about the woman's moral character. Second, many commentators express doubts

about the woman's ability to engage Jesus in serious conversation. Both strategies delegitimize the woman as a
conversation partner for Jesus and hence as a recipient of the
gospel.

(1992: 296)

In sum, her history is 'sinful and her reactions obtuse' (D'Angelo
1999: 133). This history of interpretation has distracted the question
away from the role and purpose of this key character in the Gospel.

Interpretations that present the woman as stupid or theologically
naive fail to take account of the irony and humour apparent in the
dialogue. Jesus initiates the exchange with the words, 'Give me a
drink' (4.7). This direct, or even rude, demand, lacking any formal
address, is dealt with by the woman with a flippant rejoinder.
Her reply highlights the irony in a situation where a Jew would ask
a Samaritan woman for a drink: a doubly out-of-bounds social
encounter comprising a traditional enemy and an unaccompanied
woman. Jesus takes up this sparring tone and develops the irony: 'If
you knew the gift of God, and who it is who is saying to you, "Give
me a drink," you would have asked him, and he would have given
you living water' (4.10).

The woman's next reply is not obtuse, but humorous, and
convincingly realistic within the situation, because at this point she
does not know, and could not know, that she is in dialogue with
the Son of God. She jovially points out that he would be hard pressed
to hand out this water since the well is deep and he is the one
without the bucket! She also chides him for implied lack of respect
for the history of the well: 'Are you greater than our ancestor Jacob?'
(4.12). This comment draws the Gospel readers into the irony of the
situation – they have read John 1 and know she is being addressed
by the incarnate Word of God – one certainly greater than Jacob.
Jesus' script then switches from irony to christological revelation,
presenting his own person as the source of the waters of eternal life
(4.14). Again, understandably, the woman remains unimpressed at
his lofty words and teases him: 'Sir, give me this water, so that I
may never be thirsty or have to keep coming here to draw water'
(4.15). Jesus then abruptly switches the subject to address the
woman in personal terms, asking her to call her husband. When she
replies that she has no husband, he reveals knowledge of her private
life that prompts her to believe in him to an extent that no mere
christological riddle could achieve. His observation that the man she
lives with is not her husband, and that she has had five husbands,

is made without any accompanying condemnation; indeed there is no moralising comment on this issue to be found anywhere in the story (Reinhartz 1995: 573; Conway 1999: 117). This is a silence that has been readily filled by the fantasies of successive commentators: '..."woman" tends to put her on the shelf, but the story implies that she is possibly youthful and attractive' (Marshall 1974: 68); and Duke's in less subtle vein: 'five-time loser currently committed to an illicit affair' and 'a tramp' (1985: 101–3). O'Day speculates that the woman's predicament might have come about through her falling victim to the levirate marriage system – not unlike that of Tamar (Gen. 38; see Chapter 3, this volume).

Perhaps the best approach is to follow the clues in the narrative, and these signal clearly that it is not the woman's moral standing that is central to the story, but Jesus' insight into her life and, most particularly, her reaction to his insight (O'Day 1992: 296; Conway 1999: 117–19). Jesus' insight achieves the aim that has been apparent from the outset of the dialogue, which is to engage this woman in religious discourse. Far from being ignorant, the Samaritan woman immediately refers to one of the central points of division between the Jews and Samaritans – the place designated by God for worship – and, in doing so, takes up the issue of the schism that she referred to at the very start of their encounter (4.9; Conway 1999: 119). Jesus' subsequent revelation to her concerning his true identity includes the Johannine key christological phrase, 'I am' (εγω ειμι) (O'Day 1986: 72).

At this point the disciples enter the scene. Their incredulity on discovering the encounter between their master and a Samaritan woman is reported by the narrator rather than voiced directly: 'At this moment in the narrative they are outsiders, mere observers of the scene that is taking place' (O'Day 1986: 74). The author is making a deliberate contrast between the disciples and the woman. Her readiness to listen to and to prompt Jesus about his identity and mission, her belief in him and, moreover, her immediate actions in bearing witness about him to her people, all stand in stark contrast to the hesitant disciples who cannot see beyond the potentially scandalous sight that confronts them. Their distance from Jesus is emphasised by their reported speech. Unlike the woman, they do not engage directly with Jesus. The author is using gender strategically to make the two-fold theological point about the nature of faith and the universality of Jesus' mission on behalf of God the Father. The Samaritan's gender and foreignness serve this purpose to perfection.

The author of John, in line with his own religious narrative tradition, uses the motif of the foreign woman to signal a vital theological moment: the revelation that the Messiah has appeared (4.26). Just as foreign women (Tamar and Ruth) played crucial roles in events leading to the birth of the archetypal Messiah, King David, so this woman heralds the dawn of messianic deliverance. Her lively engagement with Jesus, ending with her christological proclamation of him as the Messiah, signifies her pivotal role within this particular text. This strategy that gives such prominence to a woman's voice and her actions is reminiscent of the role given to Judith. The underlying theological purpose of these texts is similar: to allow divine redemptive power to be exercised. Inevitably, the subordination of human male instruments is included in this strategy, since men are potentially the nearest 'competitors' to divine omnipotence. In the case of the book of Judith we observed this strategy at work in relation to the characters of Holofernes, Achior and the elders of Israel (see pp. 97–8). In John's Gospel we can observe it first in relation to the earlier account of Jesus' encounter with Nicodemus. Nicodemus comes to Jesus by night, but the Samaritan woman meets him at midday, a point emphasised by D'Angelo: 'whereas he came by night and left in the dark, she comes at the point of fullest possible light' (1999: 133). We should add that what is missing from Nicodemus' encounter is any mention of subsequent witness in the light of the revelation made to him (Conway 1999: 103). This is a deliberate and remarkable silence, especially in the light of this character being given the role of audience for, perhaps, the most famous words of the Christian Bible:

> For God so loved the world that he gave his only Son, so that everyone who believes in him may not perish but may have eternal life.
>
> (3.16)

Second, this strategy is evident in relation to the disciples. We are told that many Samaritans believed (πολλοι επιστευσαν) because of this woman's witness (δια τον λογον της γυναικος μαρτυρουσης) (4.39). In contrast, Jesus confronts the unbelief of his own disciples: 'but among you are some who do not believe' (αλλ' εισιν εξ υμων τινες οι ου πιστευουσιν). His words are followed by the author's comment: 'For Jesus knew from the first who were the ones that did not believe, and who were the ones that would betray him' (6.64).

111

If we investigate John's Gospel more closely in relation to this type of strategy we see how certain characters, such as the Samaritan woman, are presented with a deliberate lack of interest in any historical reality, and instead the focus concentrates on them as symbols of idealised faith and discipleship. Another notable example is the Beloved Disciple, the anonymous witness to the Gospel (21.24), who won the race with Peter to reach the empty tomb, and who, in contrast to Peter who simply viewed the scene (θεωρει) (20.6), saw and believed (ειδεν και επιστευσεν) (20.8). While continuing the strategy of contrast, the Beloved Disciple gradually emerges towards the end of the Gospel as the perfect male disciple. Anonymity signals the true models of faith and one character that is consistently unnamed – though clearly identified – is Jesus' mother (Conway 1999: 69–85). The author resists using her name, 'Mary', a name embedded in the early kerygma, and instead refers to her as 'woman' or 'mother', carefully placing her in pivotal positions at the start and close of Jesus' ministry – at the first 'sign' at the marriage in Cana and at the foot of the cross. She is his first and last disciple.

Dorothy Ann Lee reflects on the centrality of female characters in John's Gospel – 'women are beloved in this Gospel, established through the narrative as witnesses of faith, apostolic leaders, missionaries, and proclaimers' (1999: 184) – but notes that, at the same time, they are excluded by their gender from the exclusive father/son relationship that is central to the Gospel. Lee concludes on a positive note through arguing for a symbolic interpretation of this relationship together with 'a careful deconstruction of the idolatry of gender' to 'restore women, without distortion, to the divine image and the divine embrace' (1999: 184). Such a strategy stems from a confessional need to be embraced by the divine despite the evidence of first-century exclusive attitudes to women, acknowledged by Lee (1999: 182–3). Indeed, the focus on the fatherhood of God evident in John's Gospel can explain why women play such key roles, since their gendered existence in the patriarchal societies that characterise the ancient world epitomises the type of submissive, childlike faith and obedience that is demanded by the father-God. Theological texts, such as the Gospels, that stem from such societies, can use female figures as faith paradigms without any compulsion to address or redress the actual status of women in theological, political or social terms.

The examples discussed above from the Gospels of Mark and John display how, within these texts, writers applied gender as a strategy in order to convey the radical nature and demands of the New Age that was inaugurated through the ministry of Jesus of Nazareth. They were not engaged in the task of reforming their patriarchal society, but rather they used gender in a way that illustrated the paradox that lay at the heart of the Jesus movement. This is crystallised in a teaching of Jesus, included by the author of Mark in his account of the disciples James' and John's request to sit in positions of honour beside their master when the messianic mission is accomplished:

> You know that among the Gentiles those whom they recognize as their rulers lord it over them, and their great ones are tyrants over them. But it is not so among you; but whoever wishes to become great among you must be your servant, and whoever wishes to be first among you must be slave of all.
>
> (10.42–4)

The disadvantaged social position of women within patriarchal society constantly personifies this radical humility demanded by the Gospel. The ideal lack of autonomy, or a notion of self, in human maleness culminates in the crucified figure of Christ, but this has been prefigured in the discipleship of his women followers. These paradigms are aimed within the Gospel accounts at the twelve male 'would-be' followers, and to the wider audience of male believers, that is, at those who have most to lose in the act of submission.

6

RECONFIGURING THE
BOUNDARIES

In the previous chapter we analysed archetypes of the correct modus vivendi for true believers represented by the figure of Judith in the Jewish Apocrypha and by the female followers of Jesus in the Christian canonical Gospels. The extensive period in which these texts are set is a time in history that saw the rise and intensification of political power on a scale hitherto unknown. For the Graeco-Roman world it was the time of ascendancy for the superpowers. We have seen how this can translate on the religious plane into radical expectations for a deity's adherents. But what happens to a deity caught within the arena of the superpowers? These all-powerful human agencies have visible powers that have only been imagined in the apocalyptic nightmares of prophets, and their empires' boundaries extend beyond the known world of most citizens. Such power raises the emperors themselves beyond human categories, and their apotheosis seems a somewhat natural development. For a deity to be deemed active and effective within these arenas of the ancient world, affirmation can only be supplied by acts of faith from its adherents, and the greater the challenge then the more extreme these acts become. Martyrdom can be understood within such a context. The greater the success of the ancient empires in political, cultural and social terms, then the more dire are the implications for the status of the deity and the demands on the faithful. This is the backcloth against which we should understand the nature of belief and practice encapsulated in the sacred texts that survive from those times, and, in particular, understand the canonical texts that provide the foundation for Christian belief.

FATHERHOOD – DIVINE AND HUMAN

As we have shown in the texts examined in previous chapters, the Bible contains varieties of constructions of gender that compete and contradict across the breadth of the canon. But, as we explore the question of human identity in relation to the biblical deity more critically, it becomes evident that one of the most consistent biblical images of being human is that of being infantile. Correspondingly, the pervading biblical divine image is that of parent, almost invariably that of father. The application of this familial metaphor for the divine/human relationship becomes more dominant within the literature of emerging Christianity, although, as we observed in the creation narrative and the story of Abraham (Chapters 2 and 3; see also Chapter 1), the same relationship is frequently inferred, if not articulated, in ancient Israel's religious literature.

It is surprising, looking at biblical and theological scholarship, to observe how reluctant scholars have been to tease out of the full implications of employing this familial imagery within particular contexts. Instead, the debate has focused on whether Jesus' use of the term 'abba' for God was a new theological insight and therefore distinctive to the Jesus movement and subsequent Christianity (Schrenk and Quell 1967: 984–5), or whether it was a concept at the heart of early Jewish piety (Moore 1927: 201–11; D'Angelo 1992: 617–22). The argument that it was exclusively a childish word (Shrenk and Quell 1967: 985) is unconvincing, and depends on evidence from the Babylonian Talmud rather than material that clearly dates from the time of Jesus.

The unarticulated presumption underpinning this debate was that the relational term 'father'/'abba' had a universally understood meaning. It is taken for granted that the 'childish' term inevitably conveys love, intimacy and protection. The tendency has been to take the notion of 'father' and with it the notion of being 'children' as phenomena that are ahistorical and can be applied universally. As a result they have not attracted extensive critique or merited significant deconstruction (see Chapter 1). Furthermore, if the notions of God as father and believers as children of God are offered with a plurality of meaning within the Bible itself, then such a multifaceted image would have more resonance in the wider context of a postmodern world, where new and alternative interpretations of 'being family' coexist alongside the normative one of white, colonial experience – or fantasy.

In his essay, 'Fatherhood: From Phantasm to Symbol' (1974), Paul

115

Ricoeur prefers primarily an exegetical rather than theological approach for understanding biblical notions of God as father. He offers a method of interpreting that allows for a plurality of application among biblical writers, depending on particular contexts:

> Exegesis has the advantage of remaining on the level of representation and of delivering up the very process of representation, its progressive constitution. In deconstructing theology right to its original representative elements, exegesis plunges us directly in the interplay of the designations of God, it ventures to deliver up to us their originary intention and proper dynamics.
>
> (1974: 482)

Ricoeur is referring essentially to the variety of literary contexts contained within biblical texts, but we should extend his methodology as regards the image of 'father' to an awareness of the diversity of historical contexts represented across the pages of biblical texts. Along with this diversity we can observe a historical trajectory that serves to intensify the notion of fatherhood in socio-political terms that is inevitably reflected in the theologies of the biblical writers. Ricoeur's hypothesis, which emerges from his methodology, 'designates fatherhood as a *process* rather than a *structure*, and it proposes a dynamic and dialectical constitution of it' (1974: 469). This is how familial relational biblical imagery should be read, rather than imposing on it a static understanding of fatherhood that simply mirrors contemporary ideals offering only the illusion of permanence.

First-, second- and third-wave feminist theologians, Jewish and Christian, have struggled with the exclusively male language used for the deity in foundational texts and subsequent tradition. Reformist feminist Christians have problematised the concepts of the fatherhood of God and the maleness of Jesus that infer the exclusion of the feminine, and they have suggested solutions that attempt to stay true to the religion while offering less exclusive models for God. One of the most influential scholars in this field is Sallie McFague, who offers the model of 'friend', or 'friendship', as a more constructive and inclusive metaphor for the divine/human relationship, and one that allows for human autonomy:

> Rather than stressing the protection, comfort, and redemption of individuals *apart* from others and the world, a

friendship model emphasizes sacrifice, support, and solidarity *with* others and the world. God's saving activity is
seen in an 'adult' not a 'father/child' mode. God is our friend
who suffers with us as we work with God to bring about a
better existence for suffering humanity.

(McFague 1982: 186)

Mary Rose D'Angelo is among feminist biblical scholars who have
confronted this issue, and she attempts to situate the earliest
Christian articulations of God as father within the framework of the
Roman Empire in the first century and thereby expose the limitations of such an image:

Neither Jesus nor the NT can be shown to have used the
word 'father' in a way that constitutes a transhistorical revelation that is unique and will be irreparably lost if twentieth
century theology and practice choose other imagery for God.

(D'Angelo 1992: 630)

But she warns against any simplistic attempt to drop the title 'father'
for God that takes Christianity out of the reality of its origins:

But the use of 'father' in the NT cannot be ignored; it is
important not only to diversify language and imagery for
God but also to attend to the patriarchal and imperial
horizons within which Christianity was born and has lived,
and to continue to ask how they have limited our visions
of the divine.

(1992: 630)

Diversity, or ambivalence, is certainly evident in the treatment of
the family within early Christian literature, together with the relationships and values ascribed to it. When we examine familial
attitudes within the Pauline corpus we are confronted by apparent
contradictions and tensions: there is both unequivocal teaching that
reinforces the Roman ideal of paterfamilias, and teaching that
subverts the very concept of the family unit. This particular tension
has characterised Christianity down the centuries with the paradoxical ideals of both the married state and the celibate life. Rather
than attempt to account for this inconsistency through moderating
either stance, the acknowledgement of plurality among the 'christianities' of the early period seems the more plausible explanation.

117

The early urban communities that mirrored the Roman concept of family, itself dependent on earlier ideologies (Aristotelian in particular), can be understood as visibly conforming to their social context, albeit with their God as father of the macrocosmic family of believers rather than the Emperor as metapatriarch. The communities and individuals that imitated the apostle Paul in renouncing familial blood ties in favour of the divine parent and new-found siblings 'in Christ' offered a more overt challenge to the socio-political organisation of the Roman Empire (D'Angelo 1992: 628).

For the purposes of this chapter we will examine the Pauline concept of dependence on the father-God, and explore its implications for the 'natural' family in the context of the Roman Empire. Both Romans and 1 Corinthians use the metaphor of the body to depict the organic nature of these new communities – their cohesion as corporeal bodies manifesting the experience of being 'in Christ'. This Pauline metaphor has been interpreted as a radical re-visioning of community, breaking down the hierarchy of the given boundaries of class and race, if not gender, in the ancient world, and Paul's 'rhetoric pushes for an actual reversal of the normal, "this-worldly" attribution of honor and status. The lower is made higher, and the higher lower' (Martin 1995: 96). Conversely, such an extreme understanding of the sublimation of the individual could be read as the re-imagining of societal structures in the form of extreme patriarchal control. Here the hierarchy of society, mirrored by the family in the ancient world, is not so much rejected as radically redesigned – where paterfamilias is empowered beyond the most extreme vision of any Roman paradigm.

In Roman society the family and, by extension, society was strictly hierarchical, governed by the paterfamilias who was empowered by *patria potestas*, which passed through the male line. The rule of the paterfamilias over the family and household was absolute. The extreme powers afforded to the paterfamilias by *patria potestas* included *ius vitae necisque*, the right of life and death over members of the household – a right still being referred to in the days of Constantine (*Codex Justinian* 8.46.10). In addition to this phenomenal power, and not to be confused with it, the paterfamilias always had recourse to the well-attested practice of the exposure of infants (Corbier 2001: 52–73). This practice was a longstanding Greek custom as well as a phenomenon of the Roman Empire, and the evidence from Jewish writers of the first century CE (Josephus and Philo of Alexandria), who explain that it is not a Jewish custom, attests to its practice as well as its rejection. Exposure of infants illustrates well the extreme nature of the power imbued by Roman family law on a paterfamilias:

> In principle he determined the survival or exposure to die of any child born to his wife or in his household, and his wife was powerless to protest the infanticide of a legitimate and healthy child.
>
> (Fantham *et al.* 1994: 227)

Exposure could even be used in Rome as a socio-political image to symbolise the amorality and depravity of its emperors. In the Roman historian Dio Cassius' account of events at the time of Nero's infamous act of matricide (an account that is preserved in an extract by Xiphilinus), he records how an infant was exposed in the Forum with a sign attached to it stating, 'I am not rearing you for fear you might kill your mother' (*Dio Cassius* 61.16.2, *Xiphilinus*).

The practice of exposure was not a straightforward form of infanticide, and, although obviously death could result from this act, many of the newborn babies that were exposed were rescued and adopted (Rawson 1992: 172–86). Depending on where the infant was left, such an outcome could have been the deliberate plan of the natural parents, in much the same way as the abandonment of babies occurs in our own society (Corbier 2001: 66). Whether survival or death occurs, what is made clear by this practice is the absolute nature of the paterfamilias' power. Traditionally, it was thought that a child's destiny literally lay in the hands of its paterfamilias. If he did not perform the ritual gesture of raising up the child from the ground to signal that it had joined the family, then the infant was excluded – a non-person. However, this belief has been challenged by contemporary scholars, such as Thomas Köves-Zulaf (1990), and, taking into account both literary and archaeological evidence, Corbier suggests that the instruction given to feed the infant is the moment when the infant is made a member of the family (2001: 54). This new insight does not affect the extent of the paterfamilias' power since he is the one who gives, or does not give, the instruction to nurture the child. This power, exercised in deciding the membership of the family unit, demonstrates how that patriarchal society ensured that the female prerogative, endowed by nature, to be the knowledge-keeper of the true paternity of her offspring was usurped by her husband's ultimate ruling. The paterfamilias' decision to accept or expose an infant, coupled with the law of *ius vitae necisque*, offers a picture of fatherhood that is crucially different from our own. We know bad fathers exist – we experience them – but all of us in contemporary Europe, and most of us in the world, do not experience a society that legislates for behaviour that we would universally classify as 'bad'. Yet this was the experience for those living in Graeco-Roman society at the time of the emergence of Christianity, whether or not such attitudes were acceptable within their particular culture.

It is within this context that the Pauline concept of the new community needs to be set. Paul uses familial concepts of birth and new life, and of parenting, both divine and with Paul as surrogate parent. Paul's new *deusfamilias*, a term we can adopt to accentuate the Roman context for Paul's activities and emerging theology, is a mimesis of the Roman paterfamilias – and within this new family believers remain children. As children, corporately symbolising their glorified 'sibling' Christ in one family, boundaries of class, race and gender may be abrogated, but as part of a familial body they remain under the control of the *deusfamilias*. This context allows us to see in a new light early Christian attitudes to male and female relations, martyrdom and the potential political threat of the emerging new religion of Christianity within the Roman Empire.

> A crowd was sitting around him; and they said to him, 'Your mother and your brothers and sisters are outside, asking for you.' And he replied, 'Who are my mother and my brothers?' And looking at those who sat around him, he said, 'Here are my mother and my brothers! Whoever does the will of God is my brother and sister and mother.'
>
> (Mark 3.32–5)

This teaching of Jesus from Mark's Gospel and mirrored in the early urban Pauline communities, expresses the belief that new birth as a believer abrogated family blood ties, replacing them with the new family of God. This belief is sustained into the patristic period and beyond, epitomised in the words of Jerome, written to a young widow under parental pressure to remarry: 'You are not his to whom you have been born, but His to whom you have been born again' (Jerome, *Epistula* 54.4, cited in Clark 1995: 372). In this redefined concept of family, human parenting is negated and replaced by divine parenthood, and in this process believers become children totally dependent on the divine parent: 'Truly I tell you, whoever does not receive the Kingdom of God as a little child will never enter it' (Mark 10.15). In this re-visioning of family, both Jesus and

Paul serve as wise elder siblings and as surrogates on earth for the divine parent in heaven (for example, John 12.50; see also Matt. 23.37–9).

Through this analysis early Christianity can be understood as a political counter-culture movement in opposition to the prevailing norms. Graeco-Roman society was founded on the organisation of the paterfamilias, signalled in Aristotelian ideas concerning the city state, and dominant in Rome from the time of the Republic and continuing into the Imperial period. In the early Christian belief system the institution of marriage is challenged by singleness, the family by childlessness, and paterfamilias by *deusfamilias*.

No doubt the Roman system of paterfamilias did somewhat restrict the growing-up process of the family offspring, but not to the extent evident in the new religion emerging within its Empire. In practice, because of the limited life expectancy for men, coupled with the death tolls extracted in the numerous military campaigns, many young people by the time of marriage were outside any *patria potestas* (Crook 1967: 113–22). Furthermore, Rome actively encouraged its young people to marry and create their own families – a fact clearly attested to by legislation on marriage developed during the time of Emperor Augustus (27 BCE–14 CE). This reflected an attempt in early imperial times to impose on Roman society 'good family values', as understood by the imperial household of Augustus (Fantham *et al.* 1994: 294–327). The legislation to encourage marriage, and procreation within marriage, introduced in 18 and 9 BCE, was in part prompted by a fall in the birth rate, a situation that would eventually impact on the viability of future military campaigns. As Tim Parkin explains, the primary reason for getting married was 'in order to produce [legitimate] children (*liberorum procreandorum causa*)' (2001: 221). Augustus' legislation was intended to confront the mood of disillusionment as regards the married state, common among a younger generation that preferred the attractions society offered outside stable relationships. As Suzanne Dixon comments:

> Tut-tutting about upper class resistance to parenthood became the fashion from the beginning of the Principate and women were often blamed for deliberate childlessness although it was men, not women who actively resisted Augustus' attempts to promote marriage and parenthood by legislation.
>
> (2001a: 56)

Two laws were passed by Senate to remedy the situation. The first was to restrict benefits, including inheritance rights, for men between the ages of 25 and 59 who were not married, and likewise for women between the ages of 20 and 49. The second law aimed to address the lax morality apparent in Roman society by restraining adulterous behaviour. This legislation was strengthened by a system of incentives for having children; for example, a Roman mother of three was given autonomy over her property. The same applied to Italian women outside Rome who had four children, and to women from other parts of the Empire who had five children. Correspondingly, their husbands received rapid promotion in their public careers (Rawson 1992: 7–15). Suzanne Dixon looks behind the somewhat sentimental picture of family life conjured up at the time of Augustus that aimed to produce stability at home and abroad. In its stead Dixon paints a stark and contrasting landscape: 'the exposure of children, the failure to mourn many young children, arranged marriages, violence and coldness within the family, casual divorce' (Dixon 1991: 113).

The radical new movement, Christianity, called on its adherents to abrogate former family ties, and actively discouraged them from creating their own families. Paul advises the unmarried members of the Corinthian community against marriage – unless they are unable to control their sexual appetites and, thereby, liable to be led into immoral acts:

> To the unmarried and the widows I say it is well for them to remain unmarried as I am. But if they are not practising self-control (εγκρατευονται), they should marry. For it is better to marry than to be aflame with passion (πυρουσθαι).
>
> (1 Cor. 7.8–9)

In his discussion of Paul's attitudes to sexual passion and marriage, Dale Martin argues that Paul is most anxious for his communities to avoid sexual immorality (πορνειας) (1 Cor. 7.2), but that he does not offer an alternative 'pure' form of sexual passion in its place:

> The romanticism of modern Christian (especially Protestant) attitudes about marriage – that it functions as the 'fulfilment' of divinely created and 'healthy' human sexuality, or at least heterosexuality; that it is the 'normal' outcome of love between a man and a woman; that human

beings are practically created *for it* – is strikingly, though not surprisingly, absent.

(1997: 202)

Martin's assessment of Paul's attitude to sexual relations within marriage presents a credible and convincing picture that arises out of a critical reading of Paul's social and philosophical context (1995: 212–17). However, it is a radically different understanding to that found at the centre of Francis Watson's thesis on Paul and sexuality (2000). Watson, omitting reference to Martin's research, conversely presents conjugal love within the context of Pauline community life (οικονωμια) as a central archetype for reconciled humanity, and concludes his study of the Pauline sexual ethic as follows:

> In the beginning, God saw everything that he had made, culminating in the human creature in its twofold existence as male and female – and behold, it was very good. In the agape of man and women, Eros sheds his pretensions, like the prodigal son in the far country, and returns home.
>
> (2000: 259)

Although Watson acknowledges that Paul expresses ambivalence towards marriage and family (2000: 207–9), this is not confronted as a contention to his central thesis, but rather is subsumed and lost within it.

In the light of Roman legislation and ideals for family life, intended to strengthen the power of the Empire from its foundations upwards, the early Christian attitude that rejects marriage and family can clearly be regarded in terms of political action against the state, as well as 'anti-social'. This challenge to the very foundation of the Empire deepens our understanding of the external perception of Christianity in the first three centuries. New Testament scholarship has tended to focus on the internal issues raised by this radical practice, for example by explaining it in terms of an 'interim-ethic' in relation to early Christian belief in an imminent eschatology. Analysing it from the Roman perspective highlights the political threat posed by the practices drawn from emergent Christian beliefs.

CHILDHOOD IN THE *DEUSFAMILIAS* VS.
PATERFAMILIAS

Radical dependency on God the parent also has implications for our understanding of martyrdom. In providing the ultimate paradigm for childlike dependency, Jesus obeyed the father-God, 'abba', to the extreme of death on the cross. The God of early Christian experience, like the fathers of Rome, holds the power of life *and* death over 'his' children. In examining this power relationship we can discover insights into the passive attitude recorded in the Bible and early martyrologies. Virginia Burrus identifies a process of 'self-feminization' among males in the Christian aesthetic movement of Late Antiquity: 'For men, the pursuit of Christian ascesis entailed the rejection of public life and therefore the hierarchies of office and gender; in this respect, their opponents were not far off the mark when they insinuated that male ascetics were 'feminized' through their rejection of the most basic cultural expressions of male identity' (2000: 14). Daniel Boyarin, who quotes this insight from Burrus' research, notes a parallel process evident in early Judaism: 'As a tentative hypothesis, I would offer the following: Identification with the female virgin was a mode for both Rabbis and Fathers of disidentification with a "Rome" whose power was stereotyped as a highly sexualized male' (1999: 79). Boyarin uses the term 'gender-bending' as a key to understanding the phenomenon of early Christian attitudes to Rome and to martyrdom, 'thus marking their own understanding that gender itself is implicated in the maintenance of political power' (1999: 78). If, however, the radical nature of the process of 'infanticisation' is taken seriously, at least at the earlier stage of first-century Christianity, this passivity can be better understood as symptomatic of the process of infant dependence/submission in the parent/child relationship.

The account of Perpetua's fate provides a vivid insight into the mind of a martyr, resolved to die in the Arena at Carthage, at the beginning of the third century BCE. The account of her martyrdom informs us that Vibia Perpetua was 'a newly married woman of good family and upbringing (*honeste nata, liberaliter instituta*)' (2.5; Musurillo 1972: 109). Using archaeological and textual sources to present Perpetua's story, Joyce Salisbury draws a fascinating portrait of a young woman's life as she would have been brought up and educated in a traditional and affluent Roman family in this period (1997). In the actual text – that claims to include extracts from Perpetua's diary – we can see familial ties being abrogated on two levels. First we have Perpetua's renunciation of her human father, and then the miraculous liberation she is given from the bonds of her own motherhood. Her father's final pleading with her to renounce her faith and be free encapsulates the stigma attached to those who break out of the familial mode in Roman society:

> 'Daughter,' he said, 'have pity on my grey head – have pity on me your father, if I have favoured you above all your brothers, if I have raised you to reach this prime of your life. Do not abandon me to be the reproach of men. Think of your brothers, think of your mother and your aunt, think of your child, who will not be able to live once you have gone. Give up your pride! You will destroy all of us! None of us will ever be able to speak freely again if anything happens to you.'
>
> (5.1–15; Musurillo 1972: 113)

The 'grey head' of the human father corresponds to the 'grey-haired man' in Perpetua's vision, described immediately before this visit, who calls her his child and feeds her milk. This figure subsumes motherhood within its representation of fatherhood – as the God of Hebrew scriptures remains 'male' even in the act of giving birth (Deut. 32.18). This theophany represents Perpetua's baptism, or adoption/rebirth, usurping her human father, whose subsequent pleas cannot be obeyed.

Interestingly, although Perpetua is newly-married and a young mother, her husband does not figure at all in the account. The focus, in familial terms, rests on the father/child relationship; this becomes the site for filial loyalty between the human father and Perpetua's newly-discovered heavenly father. Salisbury sees Paul's teaching on the new communities as 'families', where 'previous strangers become "brothers and sisters" of the Christian communites', continuing into Tertullian's teaching in the following century: 'Tertullian created a new genealogy in which all Christians were children of their father, God, and born "from the one womb of their common ignorance", and thus were all siblings' (1997: 72).

Perpetua is finally freed from the ties of motherhood by the miraculous premature weaning of her infant son. This allows him to be removed from her safely, minimising fears for his survival bereft of his mother. Perpetua's joy at this 'miracle' is striking in terms of her lack of parental grief on giving up a child. Instead we have a matter-of-fact account of weaning that explains the difficulties surrounding breast-feeding that women throughout the ages can readily identify with: 'But as God willed the baby had no further desire for the breast, nor did I suffer any inflammation; and so I was relieved of any anxiety for my child and of any discomfort in my breasts' (Musurillo 1972: 115). Perpetua's breasts return to their ante-natal state, and further biological transformation is imagined by her when she sees herself in a vision in masculine form (*et expoliata sum et facta sum masculus*) (Musurillo 1972: 118). I would suggest that this example of 'gender-bending' is in fact a process of 'de-sexing'. Femaleness, together with its adult functions of child-bearing and parenthood are subsumed into an undifferentiated masculinity – 'brotherhood'. In her vision Perpetua becomes as one with the *adolescentes* that she sees standing at the ready to assist her (Musurillo 1972: 118). Salisbury comments, 'The narrative of Perpetua was dominated by family attachment to the new community that had become her family' (1997: 72), and within that family she is a child once more.

The 'child's' body becomes the political locus of resistance to Rome and, through the body's total submission, the power of the father-God is demonstrated to be superior to that of the father-Emperor. The issue of sexuality in early Christianity can be clarified through highlighting the infantile state necessary for believers. The childlike state simply renders sexual activity inappropriate.

The centrality of radical childlike dependence on the parent God is evident from earliest Christian literature. The familiar text from Mark's Gospel in which Christ bids the little children to come to him has been overlaid for our own reading by nineteenth-century sentimentality. Sunday school pictures of a gentle Christ figure surrounded by rosy-cheeked eager young faces have diluted the underlying radical meaning of the text. Jesus' words are, 'whoever does not receive the kingdom of God as a little child will never enter it' (Mark 10.16). To be childlike means the believer must totally surrender their will to the parent. By means of further explanation, these words of Jesus are immediately followed in the Gospel by the story of the rich young man (Mark 10.17–22), who discovers that complete childlike dependency includes childlike detachment from material possessions. All adult responsibility, good and bad, must be surrendered. The author of Mark carefully interweaves a twofold theme within this section (10.13–31) – becoming as children, or 'infantilisation', with new found siblings in fellowship with Jesus, coupled with the rejection of blood family relationships. Here Jesus addresses the disciples as 'children' (τεχνα) (10.24), and his teaching to them at the end of the section is most explictly anti-blood family. Peter claims that he and his fellow disciples have already given up everything to follow him. Rather than affirming his close followers for their acts of renunciation, Jesus emphasises the radical nature of his gospel:

> Truly, I tell you, there is no one who has left house or brothers or sisters or mother or father or children or fields, for my sake and for the sake of the gospel, who will not receive a hundredfold now in this age – houses, brothers, sisters, mothers and children, and fields, with persecutions – and in the age to come eternal life.
>
> (10.29–30)

This passage reads like a précis of the early martyr's creed, reflecting the context of persecution in which this Gospel was written (see Chapter 5, this volume): renunciation of blood family, rebirth into the family of believers, followed by persecution and then the goal of unity with the father-God. Ultimately, the demands of dependency include the right to life itself. Jesus, the true paradigm of the believer, goes through the battle of self-will against parental will at Gethsemane, and finally submits to the demand for his life made by the father-God. His human parent, Mary, stands helpless at the foot of the cross, and the only task remaining to her is to pick up the broken body of her child. Human parenting has been overcome by the new order.

The image of the crucifixion that was equated with total defeat in human eyes is transformed by Christian theology, beginning with Paul, to be the icon of divine victory:

> We proclaim Christ crucified, a stumbling block to Jews and foolishness to Gentiles, but to those who are called, both Jews and Greeks, Christ the power of God and the wisdom of God. For God's foolishness is wiser than human wisdom, and God's weakness is stronger than human strength.'
>
> (1 Cor. 1.23–5)

The paradox of the cross exposes human judgement as inferior to divine wisdom. Humanity has to be transformed back to its original blueprint, and become the true children of God rather than divine clones (Gen.3.5). Paul readily uses the language of the Eden myth; in his theology Jesus becomes Adam, and we are called back to Eden and are expected to put the fruit of empowerment back onto the tree of knowledge.

Paul addresses the Corinthian community as his children, and admonishes them as parents would when they go against his instruction. He uses parenting imagery for his relationship with them: 'I fed you with milk, not solid food' (1 Cor. 3.2; see also 1 Thess. 2.7). This maternal imagery is even more explicit in Galatians 4.19 – 'My little children, for whom I am again in the pain of childbirth until Christ is formed in you' – and prompts Carolyn Orsiek to comment, 'Perhaps a man willing to use such an image is not as alienated from women's experience as Paul is made out to be' (1992: 336; see also Gaventa 1990). The notion of Christ being formed within believers and the apostle bringing that growth to birth is consonant with Paul's theological anthropology where the identity of the individual is subsumed into Christ, as Paul has experienced for himself: 'It is no longer I who live, but it is Christ who lives in me' (Gal. 2.20). Any notion of self is put to death, and adults become as children within the *deusfamilias* system.

Paul's parental role remains a surrogate one. He is their father figure and their nanny, conscious that God is the true parent: 'Only God gives the growth' (1 Cor. 3.7); and 'Though you might have ten thousand guardians in Christ, you do not have many fathers' (1 Cor. 4.15). He chides them as one *in loco parentis*: 'am I to come to you with a stick?' (1 Cor. 4.21). This parental role allows Paul the right to advise on the most intimate matters, including sexual behaviour. Even those who are married are not outside his remit; they are treated as children too, and advised on their sexual relations (1 Cor. 7.1–16). Although God is the true parent, bestowing life on the believers, Paul as surrogate guides them out of the waters of baptism/birth and equips them for the new-style family life.

This paradigm of divine parenting is not created by Christianity, but is a radical development of the intimate relationship between God and his elect people, evidenced in the Hebrew scriptures by the patriarchal narratives and the Israelite prophets. Israelite religion is family-centred, built on the family of Abraham, a concept readily reapplied by Paul to those who recognise the significance of Christ. Abraham and his family are crucial for understanding the nature of family to the early Christians. It is both secure and, to the outsider, dangerous (see Chapter 3, this volume). Abraham is seen in Christian eyes to be the archetypal figure of faith (Rom. 4), who demonstrated radical dependency on God by leaving his home country and travelling in faith. This journey of faith takes him through impossible family problems that climax with God's command to Abraham to sacrifice Isaac, the only child of his marriage with Sarah. This radical dependency, this submission of human will to that of God, means that Abraham obeys. The text of Genesis 22 prompts us to conclude that Abraham would have gone through with this act of infanticide if there had been no further divine intervention. Indeed, in the divine re-enactment of the scene on the Christian stage, God as father allows the killing to go ahead.

There is no doubt that the family was a potentially dangerous locus in the ancient world. When we look outside essentially early Christian literature, and its Israelite and diasporic religious heritage, to find the points of contact between emerging Christian teaching and its immediate environment, we can find convincing elucidation. Paul was a pragmatic apostle, who admitted to becoming all things to all 'men' for the sake of the gospel (1 Cor. 9.19–23). His strategy was to use language and symbols that were familiar to his communities, and then show how they might be transformed in the light of the Christ-event. Paul's social and political context was the Roman Empire. When he used familial language to his communities in the cities of the Roman Empire, the resources he was utilising were those familiar to them. This point is emphasised by Eva Lassen in her contribution to an edited collection of essays on the construction of early Christian families: 'The use of family metaphors, on the one hand, made Christianity understandable, recognisable – and, in every sense of the word, familiar to the Romans' (1997: 115). Lassen continues, however, 'The contrast, on the other hand, between the old Roman family – as an ideal and a metaphor – and the new Christian family of metaphors, must have meant that the Christian metaphorical language would have been often surprising, or even shocking to the Roman ear' (1997: 115). For Lassen, the point of departure between Roman and Christian use of familial metaphors comes with the new religion's use of this imagery to convey equality rather than authority. While there is evidence that certain articulations of early Christianity did convey a notion of the egalitarian community (expressed, for example, in the Pauline body metaphor in Romans 12 and 1 Corinthians 12), equality was relative and applied to the members or 'siblings' of the community. Although in this context hierarchical leadership did not prevail at that level, absolute authority is certainly evident at the parental/divine level – comparable to imperial notions of a *pater patriae*.

The family, or paterfamilias, was the central institution for Rome, encapsulated by the Vestal cult that contained and maintained the hearth and fire of the Empire (Beard *et al.* 1998: 51–4). The Vestal shrine, originally built more in the shape of a house than a temple, kept the home fire burning and its pantry, the *penus*, stored the sacred penates or gods. One of central and sacred duties of the Vestal Virgins was to clean the *penus* regularly and scrupulously. The Vestal shrine represented in macrocosm the family home of the Empire, and likewise the household of the Emperor underpinned the permanence of the state. The vital importance of the Vestal Virgins might tempt us to conclude that a feminine principle lay at the heart of the Roman Empire. However, the organisation of the Vestal shrine mirrored the paterfamilias structure with the Pontifex Maximus, a position held by Emperors, in charge. His mandate included meting out physical punishment to the women if the fire went out:

> The Vestals represented a peculiarly extreme version of the connection between the religious life of the home and of the community: if anything went wrong in their house, the threat was to the whole *salus* (safety) of the Roman people – not just of the city, but including the health and fertility of the whole community, its animals and its farms.
>
> (Beard *et al.* 1998: 52)

When Emperor Augustus, whose influence coincided with the period in which Christianity originated, became Pontifex Maximus he created a new, closer alignment between the priestly office and the Vesta religion. He created a new shrine dedicated to the goddess when he built his own imperial residence on the Palatine, while the original one with its sacred fire and objects remained in the Forum (Beard *et al.* 1998: 189–91). According to Ovid, with the installation of Vesta, along with Apollo, another central deity of Rome, Augustus' house contained three deities:

> Vesta has been received in the house of her kinsman; so have the senators rightly decreed. Apollo has part of the house; another part has been given up to Vesta; what remains is occupied by Augustus himself ... A single house holds three eternal gods.
>
> (*Fasti* IV.949–54; cited in
> Beard *et al.* 1998: 191)

While the Vestal Virgins stoked the Empire's home fire, the Father of the Empire, the actual title being *Pater Patriae*, 'Father of the Fatherland' (a title officially bestowed on Augustus by the Roman Senate in 2 BCE), exercised his supreme control over the global household. He was both father and – through apotheosis – god (Beard *et al.* 1998: 208–10).

The concept of the family was analogous with the concept of empire, and the imperial family was the central icon. The Augustan *Ara Pacis* ('Altar of Peace') set up in Rome is one piece of archaeological evidence from the time that epitomises the focus on familial fecundity and well-being with images of motherhood and children alongside agrarian pictures of plenty (Dixon 1988: 74–5; Beard *et al.* 1998: 203–4). Each family within the upper strata of the Empire emulated the structure. Evidence is more scarce regarding the lower strata, but there are indications that the basic paterfamilias structure was still dominant, although inevitably more limited in terms of size and wealth. The family and, by extension, society was strictly hierarchical, governed by the paterfamilias who was empowered by *patria potestas*, which passed through the male line. The rule of the paterfamilias over the family and household was absolute. We have already noted the extreme powers afforded to the paterfamilias by *patria potestas* over members of the household that included the right of life and death. He could sanction the killing of an individual within his family with or without the advice of his *concilium* – his advisers.

This Roman model for family was evident in the environment of the early urban Christian communities, and, of course, most obvious to the Roman community that lived alongside the central model – the imperial family. When Paul used terminology of the family, when he spoke of God as father, and Christ as son, the points of reference for his audiences, and for himself, would be those of Graeco-Roman society. The total obedience, described in Pauline theology, required of the son to the father-God makes sense in the context of the paterfamilias.

The religious experience offered by earliest Christianity was something quite different from what was classified as religion in the Roman Empire at that time (Beard *et al.* 1998: 214–28). In Tacitus' *Annals* (15.44) it is described as *superstitio*, not as *religio* (this distinction is reversed by the time of Constantine in the fourth century: Christianity becomes *religio* and pagan cults *superstitio*). The term *religio* is related in meaning to legislative language, and includes the meaning of 'obligation' as applied to a devotee's reasonable reverence or fear of the god or gods. The other term, *superstitio*, by contrast, describes *un*reasonable religious belief. It goes far beyond the usual remit of religious affiliation. It was by applying familial language that Christianity could radically develop its ideas, exploding the concept of religion wide open and daring to venture into every aspect of the believer's life, from 'birth' to death, and even beyond. This can be illustrated by a passage in 1 Corinthians. Paul has heard that a member of the community is living with his stepmother, acting as paterfamilias to the community/family, and Paul passes judgement and orders the man out of the 'family'. He actually writes, 'You are to hand this man over to Satan for the destruction of the flesh, so that his spirit may be saved in the day of the Lord' (5.5). Paul exercises *patria potestas*, his ultimate power of life and death over the family. The combination of religious belief and its own macrocosmic version of paterfamilias make Christianity comparable only to the phenomenon of the Empire itself.

Using the paradigm of paterfamilias we can envisage the emerging new religious movement of Christianity, as it spread into the cities of the Empire, as representing an alternative version of this foundational element of the Roman world. Although it bears similarities in structure, in its dissimilarities it can be seen as a destabilising phenomenon. The macrocosm for the family structure in the Roman world was the imperial household itself, headed by the Emperor-god, and underpinned by the constant hearth fire of Vesta. This was the overarching superstructure, which was emulated by microcosmic family units. Christianity did not simply become absorbed into this superstructure; instead it offered an alternative to it, or a rival for it. In place of the Emperor-god was the Christian God, with Christ the heir apparent, and the flame of the Holy Spirit burning, as Vesta's flames burned, in the hearts of the members of the divine household and all those living under divine *patria potestas*.

In this analysis the scenes of martyrdom described in early Christian literature provide a commentary on the power struggle between two superpowers. These scenes are microcosmic political confrontations between these superpowers, whose eventual merger in the person of Constantine can appear inevitable. In his vivid exposition of the book of Revelation, where the two superpowers are pitted against each other in epic apocalyptic imagery, Stephen Moore interchanges the figures of the biblical God and the Roman Emperor (identified as Domitian in Moore's interpretation): 'Thus it is that the deified Domitian, fortuitously fused with the figure of Yahweh, suddenly finds himself in possession of the latter's weapon' (Moore

1996: 136). The weapon the two share is the bow/rainbow (Rev. 4.5; see also Ezek. 1.28; Suetonius, *Domitian* 19).

ONENESS AND ETERNAL INNOCENCE

As we mentioned above, one feature of dissimilarity between familial structure embodied by the Empire and by Christianity regards the attitudes to marriage and children. The expectation in the imperial household and others was for children to grow up and out of the family home, to marry and form their own households, albeit remaining under the *patria potestas* of the paterfamilias until he died. In the Christian *deusfamilias*, where members of the family are discouraged from marrying, they are thereby discouraged from producing children. They remain children within the household of God, under the immediate rule of the *deusfamilias*. The divine family stands in place of the human family. New members enter this family by being born through the rite of baptism, and it is this state of being that requires closer examination.

In Wayne Meeks' milestone article, 'The Image of the Androgyne', that appeared nearly thirty years ago, he focused on the relative status of the men and women addressed by Paul, and concluded that

> [while] Paul insists on the preservation of the *symbols* of the present, differentiated order . . . these symbols have lost their ultimate significance, for 'the form of this world is passing away'. Therefore Paul accepts and even insists upon the equality of role of man and woman in this community which is formed already by the Spirit that belongs to the end of days.
>
> (1974: 208)

The belief common in contemporary hermeneutics that Paul did advocate equality between men and women stems from an understanding of Paul's concept of 'oneness' in Christ that is most clearly expressed in Galatians 3.28: 'for you are all one in Christ Jesus' (παντες γαρ υμεις εις εστε εν Χριστω Ινσου). We noted this 'oneness' earlier in relation to Lassen's work on familial metaphors in Roman society and early Christianity (see p. 129), and the positive potential this has for women's full inclusion into Christian communities is clearly articulated in Sheila Briggs' contribution on 'Galatians' to Elisabeth Schüssler Fiorenza's feminist commentary project, *Searching the Scriptures*: 'The implications of Gal. 3.28 for gender roles and status are momentous, especially when one considers how the abolition of the three sets of hierarchical relations intensified the egalitarian effect' (1995: 219). But the question of whether hierarchies are challenged by this formula – indeed whether it does offer an egalitarian vision at all – still incites lively debate among scholars. Extra-biblical evidence does tend to undermine the egalitarian interpretation. 'No longer male (αρσεν) or female (θηλυ)' (Gal. 3.28) suggests an androgynous humanity, but, as Martin comments, 'for the ancient world androgyny does not imply equality' (1995: 230); these Greek terms are precisely those used by Philo in his account of the creation of the first man. Certainly Fiorenza, an advocate of the egalitarian vision, sees in later gnostic and patristic writings a type of androgyny that has little to offer women in terms of equality: 'becoming a disciple means for a woman becoming "male", "like man", and relinquishing her sexual powers of procreation, because the male principle stands for the heavenly, angelic, divine realm, whereas the female principle represents either human weakness or evil'. But she continues, 'Gal. 3.28 does not extol maleness but the oneness of the body of Christ, the church, where all social, cultural, religious, national, and biological gender divisions and differences are overcome, and all structures of domination are rejected' (1995b: 218). Such an interpretation does seem more rooted in the idealism of liberation theology than the realities of ancient perceptions of gender and androgyny.

Dale Martin has explored the notion of becoming 'one' in the baptismal formulas and theology of Paul, and concludes, conversely, that Paul, in his context within the ancient world, presents an 'unequal androgyny' (1995: 230). Martin goes on to demonstrate that 'androgyny was invariably described in male terms' (231). In sum, redemption for a woman meant losing her female nature and being subsumed up the gender hierarchy to maleness. Martin records that Meeks 'now recognises that androgyny does not imply equality' (1995: 294, n. 4). Aristotle's view that maleness represented perfection and femaleness imperfection prevailed in antiquity and any notion of androgyny was inevitably an ideal one that sought a form of perfected humanity. To obliterate maleness would be nonsensical in this context (Gilhus 1983: 33–43), but to subsume imperfect femaleness into perfected humanity, that is, maleness, would be an imaginable ideal.

Inequality between men and women is evident elsewhere in Pauline literature – particularly in 1 Corinthians 11.2–16 and

14.34–6 (see also 2 Corinthians 11.3) – and, as Boyarin argues, Galatians 3.28 does not represent a point of departure. Boyarin understands Paul's apparent contradictory teaching on the status of men and women on two levels and, in doing so, offers a path to finding a credible consistency in his thought. Paul's acceptance of inequality within the gender hierarchy functions at the level of physical, embodied relationships. Conversely, the notion of 'oneness' for believers functions on a spiritual level: 'Paul holds that ontologically – according to the spirit – there is a permanent change in the status of gender at baptism, but insofar that people are living in their unredeemed bodies, gender transcendence is *not yet* fully realised on the social level – according to the flesh' (Boyarin 1994: 195). The spiritual 'oneness' can be clarified by drawing on Philo's account of both the ascetic, contemplative group he names the *Therapeutae* (*De vita contemplativa* 32–33 and 69; Kraemer 1992: 113–17; Sawyer 1996: 78–9), and his concept of the primal androgynous figure articulated in his commentary on Genesis 1.27, 'neither male or female' (ουτ' αρρεν ουτε θηλυ) (Philo, *De Opificio Mundi* 134; Meeks 1974: 179; Boyarin 1994: 180–200). Boyarin argues that, in the context of ecstatic worship, both the *Theraputae* and the early Christian communities known to Paul could experience moments when this spiritual androgyny could be realised – when gender was transcended (1994: 190).

What might be more significant in the current discussion is not the question of whether there is a gender hierarchy assumed by Paul, but rather the question of the status of men and women within this oneness *in relation to the deity*. In answering this question we discover that both femaleness *and* maleness are disempowered. If we begin with a comment made by Boyarin:

> From Philo and Paul through late antiquity gender parity is founded on a dualistic metaphysics and anthropology, in which freedom and equality are for pre-gendered, presocial, disembodied souls, and is predicated on a devaluing and disavowing of the body, usually, but not necessarily, combined with a representation of the body itself as female.
>
> (1994: 198)

The concept of androgyny underpinning Paul's concept of 'oneness' would have been imagined in idealised male terms on two counts. First, because human perfection was traditionally understood in those terms; and second, because the female embodied key matters of difference. Menstruation, pregnancy, childbirth and menopause enact essential differences between male and female, whereas embodied maleness can be construed as 'neutral' in the sense that the male body is not the site for birthing and its accompanying experiences. Pre-pubescent maleness is the ideal model for primal androgyny. In the Pauline image of the community, Jew/Greek, slave/free and man/woman, as 'oneness' in the body of Christ – a male body with genitalia (1 Cor. 12.23) – are all as παιδιον, or τεκνον: little children. In this neutered category neither maleness nor femaleness is significant, rather beings are sexless in that they exist only in terms of their relation to the parent.

In 'The Image of the Androgyne' Meeks utilises Encratic gnostic literature to illustrate the transcendence of gender differentiation in Pauline theology. While he saw a tension in Paul between the realities of living in the 'old' world whilst anticipating the 'new', in baptismal actions and formulas, the dissolution of gender boundaries, he argued, offered a radical equality in these early communities. He also notes, while commenting on logia in the Gospel of Thomas that are close in content to Matthew 18.1–3 and Mark 10.13–16, that:

> The *monachos* (the solitary one) in the Gospel of Thomas is clearly one who is beyond sexuality; he is like 'a little child' (logion 22), whose innocence of sexuality is portrayed in the removal of clothing without shame – like Adam before the Fall (logion 37, cf. logion 21).
>
> (Meeks 1974: 194)

Is this a significant clue to understanding the nature of oneness in Christ? The model of the child as the perfect believer is itself pre-empted in the prelapsarian human figures – the archetypes for the children of God birthed through the waters of baptism. Just as Adam and Eve can name only God as parent, the source of their being, so believers have only one parent. There is no room for alternative human parents.

Ideal humanity, not tainted by disobedience, imitate their sibling Christ, the second Adam, who is paradoxically the unique manifestation of the first Adam who bears the image of God. The Garden of Eden, presenting the idyllic picture of perfect harmony between God and his creation, and between the orders of creation – humans, animals and nature – became the blueprint for life post-'the Day of the Lord' from the time of the eighth-century prophets, to later times when it became the model for 'the World to Come' for Paul and his contemporaries. Perfect obedience along with original innocence are the vital ingredients for the creation of a perfect humanity, and together they suggest childhood as the most appropriate state for believers.

The Gospel of Thomas contains another passage, mentioned by Meeks, that again describes infancy as the appropriate mode for discipleship:

> His disciples said: When wilt thou be revealed to us and when will we see Thee? Jesus said: When you take off your clothing without being ashamed, and take your clothes and put them under your feet as the little children and tread on them, then [shall you behold] the Son of the Living (One) and you shall not fear.
>
> (Logion 37)

For the author of this text, this childlike stance evokes the memory of the first couple who were once also naked and without shame. Meeks' article also mentions Erik Peterson's examination of a number of Christian Encratite texts that describe baptism as a process of restoration to the virginal innocence of Adam, and an epiphany of Jesus at baptism as a form of a παιδιον (child) or νεανισκος (infant) (Peterson 1959: 194–6; Meeks 1974: 194). Such texts provide yet more evidence of early forms of Christianity imagining the idealised relationship between the believer and God as one of childlike dependency coupled with an innocence, or lack of individual will, that is consonant with God's original blueprint for humanity. This interpretation of the first couple inevitably undermines theologies of late modernity that prefer a grown-up Adam and Eve capable of an adult relationship, not only with their maker, but also with one another (Watson 2000: 203–4).

As Martin and others argue, the state that transcends human sexuality, the androgynous state, retains an essentially male character and is not, therefore, the hoped-for antidote to antiquity's androcentrism. This is also clearly evident in the Gospel of Thomas:

> Simon Peter said to them: Let Mary go out from among us, because women are not worthy of the Life. Jesus said: See, I shall lead her, so that I will make her male, that she too may become a living spirit, resembling you males. For every

woman who makes herself male will enter the Kingdom of
Heaven.

(Logion 114)

This does not necessarily affirm adult human maleness, but rather
the image of the innocent Adam – without sexual awareness and,
without the forbidden fruit, without autonomy. The perfected 'man'
– whether male or female – is a child.

Philo's *De Opificio Mundi* describes the 'first man' in similar terms.
In this platonic type scheme the first man epitomises the soul of
man since he was made after the image of God, whereas the second
man epitomises the physical nature of humanity since he was fash-
ioned out of clay. Of the first man Philo writes: 'He that was after
the (Divine) image was an idea or type or seal, an object of thought
(only), incorporeal, neither male nor female, by nature incorruptible'
(*De Opificio Mundi* 134). Richard Baer, commenting on this passage,
rejects the concept of androgyny as an explanation for the phrase
'neither male nor female' (ουτ' αρρεν ουτε θηλυ) and instead argues
that Philo perceives a state beyond any type of sexual differentiation, and beyond any polarity – even that which co-exists in one
being (1970: 32–5).

At the conclusion to this section in Philo, where he speculates on
the idyll of original innocence, we find a hint of the universal experience of childhood: 'Such is the life of those who at the outset are
in enjoyment of innocence and simplicity of character, but later on
prefer vice to virtue' (*De Opificio Mundi*.170). In setting the Gospel
of Thomas against the background of Philo, and noting the lack of
specifically androgynous language in that text, Risto Uro suggests
that the Gospel of Thomas 'envisages the original realm of asexu-
ality as the final goal of human life' (1997: 222).

Paul readily uses edenic imagery to explain the new order instigated by Christ (Rom. 5; 1 Cor. 15). Christ is the new Adam – or
the true Adam, as Karl Barth suggests (1956: 513) – the worthy
son of God, in contrast to the Adam depicted in Genesis 2–3. This
picture of return to original innocence, compounded by language of
familial relations central to the earliest Christian theologies, and
clearly evident in the nature of the demands Paul exhorted to those
'in Christ', prompts us to see believers as they emerge from the
birthing waters of baptism as newborn children of God. All are
transformed into divine likeness through the imitation of the first
born, Christ, 'to be conformed to the image of his Son, in order that
he might be the first born within a large family (Rom. 8.29, NRSV

translation; or 'among many brothers' (εν πολλοις αδελφοις)). The key feature in the Pauline corporate scheme of original innocence is its preoccupation with the total submission of siblings to the will of the father-God. Paul's theology focused on the cross as the means of salvation, and he exhorts the newborn in Christ to imitate the obedience of the family's first-born – even to the point of death: 'Let the same mind be in you that was in Jesus Christ . . . being found in human form, he humbled himself and became obedient to the point of death – even death on the cross' (Phil. 2.5–8).

As the various manifestations of Christianity develop in the second and third centuries this attitude of embracing new birth in the family of God and thereby renouncing the human family, and with it the expectations of adulthood, intensifies, particularly within Gnostic and Montanist groups. As we noted above, extant texts from the late second and early third centuries provide vivid evidence of this trend of renunciation – both in terms of blood family and adulthood. The Acts of Thecla (preserved within the apocryphal Acts of Paul), dating from the second century, illustrate, in similar vein to the account of Perpetua, this a-familial attitude that rejects blood family in favour of the divine family. Thecla leaves her family behind and postpones her 'coming of age' by dramatically escaping from her arranged marriage – much to the chagrin of her mother and fiancé. The decision to dress up in male apparel is not so much an act of 'gender-bending' as further illustration of her rejection of adult female sexuality. In the case of Perpetua, as well as rejecting her human father, her adult sexuality also had to be rescinded – embodied in the existence of her infant child. Miraculously, as Perpetua eagerly anticipates martyrdom her child is weaned. She can hand over her infant child and be free to offer up her life and thus demonstrate her radical obedience to her new paterfamilias, God. Her companion Felicitas is pregnant as she awaits martyrdom. This state too is remedied in order to allow the evidence of human ties and adulthood to be removed. She gives birth early, at eight months, gives the baby away, and enters the arena unfettered (Musurillo 1972: 123–4). The demands of the deusfamilias were absolute. The greatest sign of filial love was willingness to sacrifice life itself with the reward of greater integration with the father-God in the heavenly domus.

This analysis focuses on one strand within pluralistic early Christianity, which, as we have seen, is apparent in the earliest literature, and which continued down the centuries. Another, contrasting, strand is also evident in early texts that contain the household codes.

These offer teaching on appropriate behaviour within Christian, human families, and, although Fiorenza would argue that this strand of Christianity, this 'patriarchalizing' trend, 'is not yet found in the first century' (1995b: 278), the thesis that a wide variety of 'christianities' were evident from earliest times is more convincing. Less convincing is Fiorenza's version of 'the church' – a monolithic entity that evolves in chronological fashion (1995b: 278). The biblical texts that contain the household codes (Ephesians 5–6, Colossians 3–4 and 1 Peter 3) advise husbands on how they should manage their households and treat their wives, children and slaves, and, conversely, how members of the household should love and respect its head. These codes presuppose a natural order within the family that is God-ordained. This hierarchical structure is very close to the basic structure of the paterfamilias. There has been the tendency in New Testament scholarship to see the type of Christianity represented by the household codes as the type that conforms to Graeco-Roman society, whilst the other strand, which represents a-familial teaching, is what is distinctively new in the ancient world. What I have attempted to show in this chapter is that such an explanation is oversimplified. In fact, the a-familial strand of early Christianity conforms more radically to the paterfamilias pattern. Within, for example, the early Pauline communities, although blood ties and marriage are renounced, they are replaced by the even greater demands for obedience, control and single-minded devotion from the father-God. Paul encourages the members of the community in Corinth not to marry: 'the unmarried man is anxious about the affairs of the Lord, how to please the Lord, but the married man is anxious about the affairs of the world, how to please his wife, and his interests are divided' (1 Cor. 7.32–4). Within these communities the powerful paradigm of the crucified son is central, and the demands of the deity are reinforced by the surrogate 'fathers' of the communities. Yes, there is an egalitarian spirit among these communities, but this would be expected among children of a household: the paternal authority remains firmly in place.

7

LAST THINGS

So far we have discussed the biblical texts without paying much attention to what is perhaps their most vital ingredient: their eschatological dimension. Paul, together with the evangelists who produced the Gospels, and including the Montanist movement that prompted the early martyrologies and texts such as the Acts of Thecla, all shared a common conviction that they were participants in the final chapter of God's created world order. This final chapter to the history of the world had already been described by Israel's prophetic tradition, and, for some interpreters, was even anticipated in the Bible's first chapter: the creation story.

As we discussed in Chapter 3, the Bible contains examples of normative boundaries being broken by God, who is unconstrained by any socio-political behavioural expectation. The 'end time' presents us with other anarchic images instigated by the deity on a cosmological scale that necessarily impact on human behaviour. Within the popular imagination of early Judaism during the Second Temple period, the 'end time' – characterised by judgement and subsequent renewal – would be heralded by the return of the Spirit of God, particularly in terms of its prophetic power. The book of the prophet Joel contains an inclusive image of eschatological renewal:

> Then afterward I will pour out my spirit on all flesh; your sons and your daughters shall prophesy, your old men shall dream dreams, and your young men shall see visions. Even on male and female slaves, in those days, I will pour out my spirit.
>
> (2.28–9; Hebrew text 3.1–2; see also
> *Numbers Rabbah* 15.25)

This text was used by early Christians to authenticate their charismatic experiences in terms of divine agency and to confirm that they were already anticipating the fruits of the new age (Acts 2.16–21).

The final chapter for the first Christians is believed to open with the second entrance of Jesus the Messiah onto the world scene, and most significantly the key interim action of God has been Jesus' resurrection from the dead. This was the clear signal that the final stage had begun: he is 'the first fruits of those who have fallen asleep/died' (απαρχη των κεκομημενων) (1 Cor. 15–20). Believers await their soteriological transformation that will be completed on the Messiah's return to earth, when he will complete the redemptive work begun during his earthly ministry, including the defeat of all God's enemies. Indeed, Paul, at least at one stage in his life, believed that he would be living still when this cataclysmic cosmological event would occur:

> For the Lord himself, with a cry of command, with the archangel's call and with the sound of god's trumpet, will descend from heaven, and the dead in Christ will rise first. Then we who are alive (ημεις οι ζωντης), who are left, will be caught up in the clouds together with them to meet the Lord in the air; and so we will be with the Lord forever.
>
> (1 Thess. 4.16–17; see also 1 Cor. 15.51)

This imminent eschatological dimension that permeates many early manifestations of Christianity allows for a parallel stratum of experience for believers. They were also part of the present, or 'old', world order, while already participating in aspects of the new. Paul's concept of the community as a living organic unity allows for the translation of those individuals to an alternative reality as the body of Christ. Both baptism and the eucharistic meal trigger this reality: dying with Christ in the waters of baptism, they rise up in the hope of mirroring his resurrection (Rom. 6.3–4); and through eating the body and blood of Christ they are mystically one with Christ – being in Christ and Christ in them (1 Cor. 11.23–32). Many scholars believe Paul is quoting a baptismal formula in Galatians 3.28 (Meeks 1974), while others argue for an inextricable connection between the theology contained in it and Paul's rhetoric to the Galatians (Kahl 1999: 58–9). What is of significance is that Paul opted to use this formula, whether or not he composed it, to underline his theology, and that it alludes to this alternative dimension for believers who are in Christ. Within the community,

as prophesied by the book of Joel, the end of the 'old' order is anticipated, and with it go its racial, social and gender boundaries.
Whether existence, in the form of the 'oneness' that Paul describes,
is subsumed into androgyny or maleness is tangential to the vision
of 'sameness' (see Chapter 6). This notion of 'sameness' goes beyond
theological terms and should be understood as a political strategy,
as Elizabeth Castelli argues: 'Group unity rewrites the perspective
of the dominant in the group as the perspective of the entire group,
competing discourses are replaced by a univocal discourse' (Castelli
1991: 132). This astute observation underlines the central theme of
the previous chapter, where unity amongst fellow siblings was
shown to offer a limited equality, but one that is swamped by
the dominance of the *deusfamilias*. Within that limited concept of
freedom and lack of limits, however, radical alternatives to the rigid
socio-political strata were being performed and sanctioned – but
always with a particular eschatological perspective at the forefront.
Although functioning within the borders of divine omnipotence,
female believers could reject marriage and childbearing – a radical
and anarchic concept for the Roman Empire, and for subsequent
times.

As we have argued throughout this volume, the dominant char-
acterisations of the omnipotence of God that we encounter in the
Hebrew and Christian scriptures are inevitable in the light of the
socio-political contexts that produced these texts. The Bible consistently represents a power structure that cannot be compromised,
whether God is conveyed as the benign figure heading a form of
love patriarchalism, or an all-demanding father who desires the
ultimate sign of obedience from his offspring. Any notion of egali-
tarianism or democracy is inappropriate in the context of divine will,
and absolute trust in the rightness of that will is the only appropriate response. Does this observation mean that these texts should
be rejected, and can be relevant only for those who wish to abandon
autonomy? It is, perhaps, the eschatological dimension that offers
an alternative world-view that might not be in opposition to the
postmodern/post-colonial framework of our own experiences.

Transcendent, omnipotent concepts of the deity do expose
the dichotomy that exists between the pre-modern world and the
post-Enlightenment era, and within contexts of modernity and postmodernity where autonomous individuals negotiate their own
concepts of the divine – often in terms of immanence rather than
transcendence. Contemporary critical stances tend to fall into two
camps: those who attempt to bridge the dichotomy by diluting the

archaic power structures inherent in these texts, and those who, conversely, simply reject the biblical discourse – and the traditions of Judaism and Christianity along with it. An alternative approach for those of us who wish to engage with these texts is to accept their limitations for addressing our own world, but at the same time to explore the examples they contain for challenging boundaries and for anarchic behaviour in relation to power structures. Within these subversive paradigms, or examples of '*dis*continuity' (Butler 1990: 141), we can find a striking anticipation of our postmodern world. Amongst other settings, these 'counter' discourses often emerge from biblical utopian speculation – the post-eschaton idylls that evolve prelapsarian paradise beyond the restricted lens of the Genesis depiction.

Negation of the notion of gender as constructed by a person's biological sex is a central aspect of postmodernity's rejection of metaphysical truths. Both Butler and Wittig argue that compulsory heterosexuality is rooted in the foundational power structure of our culture, and a theory of gender that transcends biological difference can allow for alternative sexualities. As we discussed in Chapter 2, applying 'heterosexual' or 'homosexual' as an individual identity marker makes no sense in antiquity, instead particular actions are defined in those terms. An individual may perform these acts, which may or may not challenge ancient societies, but this behaviour is not subsumed into an individual's essential identity. In biblical texts there are instances where gender is presented as a set of actions that function at the level of performance rather than essence (see Chapter 5), and this possibility can be utilised in the depiction of existence within God's sovereignty, particularly at the 'end time'.

GENDER-BENDING AS AN ESCHATOLOGICAL 'TOOL'

Butler's observation of consistent discontinuity throughout recorded history can be identified with the biblical portrayals of anarchy – for example, 'My people – children are their oppressors, and women rule over them' (Isa. 3.12a). Less value-laden texts that seem to reflect this radical concept of gender include Deuteronomy 32, where God 'himself' is depicted in parental terms that transcend traditional gender and biological categories. In verse 6 the deity is identified as the father of the nation: 'Is he not your father, who created you, who made you and established you?' But that narrow, human category is burst open by maternal imagery introduced in verse 18: 'You were unmindful of the Rock that bore you; you forgot the God who gave you birth.' In this verse we are presented with the unique occurrence of the verb 'to bear' in the third person masculine יָלַד. Biological restrictions evident in the created world are non-existent for the deity, and, furthermore, gender roles determined by biology can be suspended for humans when they are implementing divine plans or as a literary strategy to reflect the extremity of certain situations. For example, Deborah the Judge of Israel leads her army into battle, but, although her leadership is affirmed by God, the oddity of a woman instructing the Israelite armies stands as a signal pointing to the anarchic events that will occur as the narrative of Judges unfolds. This signal is picked up by later Jewish and Christian commentators to question why no man was available for this role, a point that neatly illustrates the process of 'gender *eis*egetics' in the history of interpretation. Through her various disguises the figure of Judith presents us with another example: as a seductress she conceals her divinely inspired role as Israel's warrior and executioner (see Chapter 5).

One passage from Jeremiah provides a fascinating example of biblical gender experimentation occurring within the context of eschatological breakdown and reconstruction. Such a re-visioning resonates with postmodern gender theory, and, viewing the text from this angle, we discover that the Bible can be illustrative, and perhaps even effective, in terms of a variable notion of gender. Judith Butler's claim that it is within the exceptional performances of gender that the ideal polarities of the gender spectrum are undermined throws light on the truly radical nature of biblical apocalyptic images of a new world order:

> The abiding gendered self will then be shown to be structured by repeated acts that seek to approximate the ideal of a substantial ground of identity, but which, in their occasional *dis*continuity, reveal the temporal and contingent groundlessness of this 'ground'.
>
> (1990: 141)

The book of Jeremiah contains an illustration of such a discontinuity: 31.22b contains the phrase, 'a woman encompasses a man' (NRSV translation). Like many biblical phrases that attract the NRSV footnote convention 'Heb uncertain', these words from Jeremiah have a long and varied history of interpretation and translation. Our justification in adding even further to the list of commentators is that this is a particularly fascinating phrase for contemporary hermeneutics as they relate to gender theory. Both this phrase and an earlier one in chapter 30, which has been used by commentators to clarify 31.22, seem to describe anarchic chaos in terms of blurred gender roles:

> Ask now, and see, can a man bear a child? Why then do I see every man with his hands on his loins like a woman in labour? Why has every face turned pale?

> (30.6)

These two verses, 30.6 and 31.22, which appear respectively at the beginning and end of a recognised literary unit, can be understood as the counter-face of patriarchal society, where the norm is for men to dominate and women to obey. In the biblical context this is epitomised in God's words to Eve regarding her relationship to Adam: 'he shall rule over you' (Gen. 3.16b). To conjure up the cosmic implications of the Day of the Lord, the author of Jeremiah can imagine the suspension of the God-ordained sexual hierarchy. In the Genesis passage, in the first part of 3.16, God tells of the pain women will experience when they give birth, and, conversely, the Jeremiah passage experiments with the anarchic notion of men dreading that same pain. The link with Genesis is linguistically implicit through the use of the Hebrew noun זכר, 'male', in the phrase, 'Can a man (or male) bear a child?' This is the noun used in Genesis 1.27 to denote the male form of the human species, in contrast to נקבה, 'female'. At the end of this literary unit, 31.22, the female, נקבה, 'encompasses' the man, further undermining the predetermined and divinely ordained roles of the sexes.

The account given above presupposes many points about a notoriously ambiguous text. It presumes that the subtext is about societal power-relations, and that obvious links exist both between these two passages from Jeremiah, and between them and the Genesis creation narrative. It serves, however, to signify the possibilities of applying these biblical phrases to illustrate contemporary gender debate and related issues in the context of postmodernity. Central biblical themes can be understood to validate a patriarchal society whose notions of gender are prescribed biologically, that is, where biology is destiny. This identification of biological sex with gender roles is clearly articulated from the start. Whatever the relationship between the first woman and the first man might have been before the forbidden fruit was taken, by the end of the episode the reader is assured that a patriarchal hierarchy is firmly in place for the subsequent biblical narrative. Furthermore, by situating this matter within the primary site of the creation narrative, it serves as a clear point of reference for levitical legislative prescriptions for male and female behaviour.

If we presume to understand Genesis 3 in terms of a 'metanarrative', providing the construct for male and female behaviour, then a description of the breakdown of these gender boundaries can be interpreted as anarchic. This tendency is evident in the NEB translation of Jeremiah 31.22b: 'For the Lord has created a new thing on the earth: a woman turned into a man.' In a postmodern context we are not bound to a dualistic value system. Terms such as 'anarchic' or 'antisocial' become meaningless or merely subjective, rather than objective reality. Applying a postmodern hermeneutic allows us to read biblical images of anarchy as alternative modes of reality set alongside those that predominate. To use Butler's phraseology, we focus on the 'occasional *dis*continuity', and, in doing so, we uncover a biblical strand that radically undermines traditional gender polarities.

When we encounter the images from Jeremiah 30.6 and 31.22b we can allow ourselves to be presented with an alternative performance of gender roles. The effect of the text is even more far-reaching, since the first passage suggests the overturning not only of societal constructed gender forms, but also of biological function. Men are functioning as biological women in experiencing the pains of childbirth.

We can justify our recourse to the creation narrative to find an explanation of these images, since Genesis is a key resource for the author/s of Jeremiah. Jeremiah 4, for example, resounds with echoes of creation of the physical world, albeit now in the process of apocalyptic un-creation. Chapter 31 itself invokes the inauguration of the circumcision covenant from Genesis 17, again transforming that phenomenon. This is achieved by internalising the process, through the notion of God's ethical imperatives being inscribed on the hearts of his people. A new relationship with God is envisaged that transcends the male exclusivity of the traditional practice of male circumcision. Our two verses might be read in a similar way.

Using Genesis imagery as the starting point, or a means to invoke a sense of familiarity on the part of the reader, the author then takes the familiar and transforms it through a reversal process. We know from Genesis that, as a result of her disobedience, Eve must suffer pain in childbirth and be ruled over by her husband. This is the familiar situation. In the section Jeremiah 30.4–31.22 the great and terrible Day of the Lord is rehearsed, and it is within the opening and concluding stanzas that we encounter the apparent challenge to traditional gender expectations. It is a day the unrighteous should dread, but it is a day of hope for the remnant of Israel. The author explodes the boundaries of natural experience with the image of a man in the agonies of labour to dramatise the extremity of human fear on that day. The curse of Eve becomes the curse of Adam in this attempt to conceptualise the end of created order: 'It is the transformation, even the transmogrification, of the normal patterns of life which characterise this particular day' (Carroll 1986: 574). The mood of this section develops from one of fear and dread portrayed at the beginning to one of redemptive hope by the end. Interspersed are pictures of the intimate and unique relationship the faithful remnant of Israel shares with its God, 'for I have become a father to Israel, and Ephraim is my firstborn' (31.9b). It is in this climate of divine promise that the second 'gender challenging' stanza occurs. Hence this is not presented as a picture to instil fear, but part of the new hope, the new creation that comes at the culmination of the Lord's Day. At the beginning of the Jeremiah section labour pains evoke the sad ending of the creation narrative, where the early promise of utopia was spoiled by the disobedient couple, and this serves to parallel the advent of another time of punishment on the Lord's Day.

These observations concerning the opening verses to this section help us throw light on the meaning of the final verse. Jeremiah 31.22b has attracted much attention from scholars, and is described by Carroll as 'perhaps the most difficult half-line in the book of Jeremiah' (Carroll 1986: 601; see also McKane 1996: 806–7). The half-verse reads, 'For the Lord has created a new thing on the earth: a female תסובב a man', and the problem lies with the translation of תסובב. This phrase deliberately invokes Genesis 1, first, by selecting the verb ברא, distinctive for God's creative activity in the opening chapter of the Bible; and second, by using the noun נקבה, female, the same noun that is used in Genesis 1.27. Like the author of Isaiah, Jeremiah looks to the creation paradigm as a source for the redemptive conclusion to the great and terrible Day of the Lord. The following verse from Isaiah describes the reawakening of the creator God:

I am about to do a new thing; now it springs forth, do you
not perceive it? I will make a way in the wilderness and
rivers in the desert.

(Isa. 43.19; see also Isa. 48.7)

Commentators have noted connections with Jeremiah 30.6 and
31.22, as well as the creation story (Holladay 1989: 195; see also
Holladay 1966, and Phyllis Trible understands Genesis 1.27 as the
clue to understanding the whole section of Jeremiah 31.15–22
(1978: 48).

The phrase 'a female תסובב a man' has an interesting history of
interpretation. Jerome understood it as the Virgin enclosing the
Christ-child in her womb. Calvin interpreted it in militaristic
terms, justified by the appearance of the noun גבר, which, in some
biblical contexts, refers to male warrior figures. He sees the weakness
of the warriors taunted as 'women' in 30.6 being later transformed,
and these 'women' ultimately becoming victorious. Contemporary
scholarship has been aware that the meaning of this phrase might
well lie in the reversal of the Genesis prescription for gender roles.
Holladay comments, '"a female shall encompass a hero", suggests
that the female shall be the initiator in sexual relations' (1989: 195).
Trible notes the use of גבר with its macho overtones, and sees it as
a device to intensify the image: 'The nuance itself, rather than its
military applications, participates in our poetic context to enhance
further the radical reversal that is the new thing of the poem' (1978:
49). Trible's exegesis is intended to demonstrate that the passage
she identifies as a unit (Jer. 30.15–31.22) is a sustained image of
female emotional and biological imagery: 'the very form and content of the poem embodies a womb: woman encloses man' (1978:
50). This image extends to the divine person through the use of רחם
in Jeremiah 31.20 to signify God's motherly (or 'wombly') compassion for the beloved child, Ephraim. Having taken the reader
through the unit identifying the extensive use of this female imagery, Trible demonstrates how the enigmatic phrase at the end of
31.22 falls into place as a concise summary of the unit's intention.
The militaristic interpretation proffered by other commentators
seems strikingly out of place beside Trible's reading of radical
female compassion.

Trible's exegesis intends to draw attention to positive applications of female imagery in biblical texts that are often neglected.
She draws our attention to the contrasting female imagery within
verse 22 itself. The negative adjective השובבה, 'backturning' or

'apostate' ascribed to Israel, here a young virgin, is contrasted to the active woman who surrounds a man, the 'new thing' created by God.

Trible notes that the female is the subject of the verb to surround: 'But to encompass is to surpass. The verb *surround* contributes to its subject *female* a power that moves beyond comparable images in the poem' (1978: 48). To take this a stage further and examine the nature of this power, we should enquire whether this is female appropriation of male power. The clues are in the text. We are told that the Lord has created a new thing on the earth, prompting the hearers to move beyond given categories and given modes of behaviour. Robert Carroll suggests that the image of the woman encircling the man can be understood as 'perhaps "the vagina envelops the penis"' (1986: 602). He sees it as a sign of regeneration:

> when Yahweh acts creatively women will be women and men will be men – and ever the twain shall meet and become one flesh! Hence the repopulation of the community.
>
> (1986: 602–3)

If it is simply a description of the resuming of normative sexual behaviour, what is 'new' about it?

The verb 'create' takes us back to the God-given origins of gender play to the time when Eve played away from the divine prescription and was destined to remain under the rule of Adam. Eve's punishment was twofold: first, to have pain in childbirth (Gen. 3.16a), an image explicitly parodied in Jeremiah 30.6 when it is transferred to male experience at the advent of the Day of the Lord. The Israelites' fear as they anticipate the wrath of God, imaged as female pain in childbirth, proves unfounded as Jeremiah presents the 'end time' instead as a process of healing and restoration for his beloved people.

Second, returning to the fate of Eve, she was to be ruled over by her husband (Gen. 3.16b). In Jeremiah this image of male domination is subverted by the 'new thing' that is to be created by God on the Day of the Lord. The verb תסובב, in the phrase 'a נקבה (woman/female, as in Genesis 1.27) shall encompass a man', is not simply an example of role reversal, of female dominance in place of male. This is the conclusion reached by the medieval Jewish commentators, illustrated by Rashi who concludes that role reversal lies behind this phrase: 'A woman shall go after a man and seek him out that she may marry him'(cited in McKane 1996: 806).

In more positive vein, this phrase actually presents a new paradigm for relations between the sexes. The newness comprises, first, the female becoming the subject, and, second, the nature of the relationship expressed in the verb תסובב that contrasts with the verb 'to rule', מָשַׁל, used in Genesis 3.16. תסובב is found in Deuteronomy 32.10 and its usage there helps to illuminate the meaning in Jeremiah: 'he (God) shielded him (Jacob) (יסבבנהו), cared for him'; it is also found in Psalms 32.10: 'but steadfast love surrounds (יסובבנו) those who trust in the Lord'. In both contexts the verb expresses the action of loving care, a divine action directed at God's chosen people. This action in Jeremiah becomes female action directed at a male object. The noun used for 'man' here is גבר. This noun carries strong macho connotations in biblical usage. It is used, for example, in Deuteronomy 22.5 in the prohibition against cross-dressing: 'A woman (אשה) shall not wear a man's apparel, nor shall a man (גבר) put on a woman's garment.' Another example appears in the Song of Deborah in Judges 5, where Sisera's mother imagines the war heroes' exploits at the end of the battle with the Israelites: 'Are they not finding and dividing the spoil – a girl or two (literally, 'a womb (רחם) or two') for every man (גבר) . . .?' (5.30). In Jeremiah this macho man is now to be encompassed in a woman's protective care.

In the opening and final stanzas of Jeremiah's imagining of the Day of the Lord, gender performance provides the means of expressing both the utter terror at the destruction feared at the start of that day, and its hope and reconstruction when God's role transforms from destroyer to creator. In the first picture men experience pain that is specific to women. But this 'crossing over' in biblical terms, as in the case of radical feminist identity theory, is a possibility since this aspect of being woman is not essential to the first Eve. The pain in childbirth is not part of her original creation, but is a feature of subsequent revision. In the prophet's catastrophic anticipation of judgement at the end of time, the punishment of Eve extends to the sons of Adam.

The last stanza also takes us back to creation – this time to envisage something new: where Adam once ruled over Eve, now Eve encircles Adam. In this new relationship hierarchical domination disappears. Instead the word 'encircle' appears and represents a female role in terms of active protection and care, offered elsewhere in biblical contexts by God. This image is novel and starkly contrasts the model of male domination that characterised male/female relations in Genesis 3. Gender roles are not fixed, but can be surpassed in biblical imagery, albeit at the end of time. Furthermore, this image affirms an adult mode of being human in contrast to both prelapsarian Adam and Eve, and the type of redeemed humanity suggested by early Christian models that entail a process of infantilisation (see Chapter 6, this volume). The 'new thing' in Jeremiah's image offers an alternative to the twofold punishment of Eve. It offers different roles for women and men to perform in the final scene of God's script for humanity.

WORKING WITH THE EXCEPTIONAL

The overriding biblical model for the divine/human relationship characterised by omnipotence and dependency respectively is consistently evident, despite the diversity of literary genre and the vast time-span that comprises the biblical period. Since the Enlightenment and humanity's, or rather man's, coming of age, this 'meta-model' has functioned as a challenge to human endeavour with the resulting, and inevitable, alternatives of either rejection or the production of various hermeneutical stances that apply exegetical tools to strip away the Bible's essential bold dynamic. Are there any biblical paradigms that might serve a humanity that has come of age? The Jeremiah passage examined above does present the possibility for men and women to encounter one another in a manner that does not replicate in microcosm the macrocosmic hierarchical divine/human relationship characterised by dominance. In biblical terms this paradigm is offered only as a utopian image, and it will remain unrealised until the end of history. This does not restrict the possibility of its application within contemporary notions of human relationships if there is meaningful resonance with particular contexts. Certainly, the Jeremiah passage presents an image of male/female partnership that reflects the contemporary western expectations of many men and women, as opposed to notions of hierarchical 'headship' or 'rule' that we encounter in other biblical material. Application of biblical texts cannot be universalised, and many social, cultural and political contexts would not resonate with this notion of male/female relations. Universal application of biblical ideas and meaning has rightly been abandoned in the postmodern context of present-day biblical studies.

The 'end time' gives permission to biblical writers to explode expectations and transgress given boundaries. Here worlds can be un-created and re-recreated, humanity can be re-gendered as well as re-generated. In this ultimate power statement of the deity the unimaginable is imagined. In an attempt to explicate biblical material that reflects the relativities of our own time, we can take eschatological speculation as a starting point for searching out the unconventional. The notion of 'discontinuity' can be applied as a methodology to reconstruct alternatives to given power structures.

Such an approach draws on the subversive element in Luce Irigaray's interpretation of 'mimesis' where parody can function within deconstructive and constructive strategies (see Chapter 1). Irigaray uses mimesis to evolve an alternative notion of 'becoming' woman, distinct from the masculine realm of discourse that names 'her' as the other, but that distinction begins with engaging with the given category 'woman' so that, through its parody, woman, as subject, not object, creates herself. If we translate this process to the biblical world-view, alternative notions of being human emerge that are in antithesis to the given divine/human relationship, but subsist within it. As such they work mimetically within the text. Biblical eschatological passages use a comparable strategy: the book of Isaiah invokes a pastoral scene, but subverts it with the image of the lion lying down with the lamb, and that of the child playing over the asp's nest. Recognising this strategy at work in the authors' attempts to evoke cosmological upheaval that goes beyond experience, we can 'work back' through the texts to discover evidence outside the eschatological realm.

Within the creation narrative we can see newly-created humanity develop into a relationship of contestation with the divine, and as such represent a parody of divine intentionality. Adam and Eve are created according to a blueprint that excludes autonomy, but subvert the divine pattern by deliberately opting for an alternative. They remain recognisable as the created 'other' to the divine, but exist as a parody, or mimesis, of the humanity intended by God. Eve, the instigator of the subversion, presents the greatest parody of all. Created as an afterthought to Adam, as his helper in the process of procreation, she emerges as the initiator. The object, the 'other' not only to God but also to man, becomes the subject who acts and allows the emergence of another type of humanity. Her action of taking the forbidden fruit exposes a level of subjectivity that had been hidden within her – disguised by her identity as the 'other' and the very mode of her creation. Her autonomy, her subjectivity, displays a way of being human that parodies the feminine role that had been prescribed for her and, in Irigaray's terms, she becomes woman by and of herself:

Beneath all these/her appearances, beneath all these/her borrowings and artifices, this other still sub-sists. Beyond all these/her forms of life or of death, still alive.

(cited in Schor and Weed 1994: 50)

So when the woman saw that the tree was good for food, and that it was a delight for the eyes, and that the tree was to be desired to make one wise, she took of its fruit and ate; and she also gave some to her husband, who was with her, and he ate.

(Gen. 3.6)

Carefully hidden by centuries of misogynist interpretation, the secret of Eve's wisdom can be revealed, and through her initiative we can discover the blueprint for autonomous humanity. Such autonomy is clearly recognised by previous generations of Christian theologians, but its dangerous implications, both social and political, particularly in relation to its manifestation in female form, ensured that it was declared devil's work and consigned to be the antithesis of perfect humanity. This position is exemplified in the sermon delivered by Tertullian in the late second century:

God's judgment on this sex lives on in our age; the guilt necessarily lives on as well. You are the Devil's gateway; you are the unsealer of that tree; you are the first forsaker of the divine law; you are the one who persuaded him whom the devil was not brave enough to approach; you so lightly crushed the image of God, the man Adam; because of your punishment, that is death, even the Son of God had to die. And you think to adorn yourself beyond your 'tunics of skins' [Gen. 3.21].

(*On the Dress of Women*, cited in
Clark 1984: 39)

Eve's initiative ensures that humanity does step out of the herbaceous playpen we mentioned earlier (see Chapter 3), but, in biblical terms, this coming of age represents an act of rebellion. Dependent and obedient, prelapsarian Adam and Eve remain the ideal. Understood as a positive initiative, Eve's action presents a biblical paradigm for human behaviour that does not resist autonomy, and allows an engagement between the text and the myriad ways of being human manifest in the modern world. On the theological level

such a reading of Eve allows for a deity that dares to risk the liberation of his creation, rather than one who knowingly creates a
defective, or potentially defective, humanity.

In an earlier chapter we discussed the character of Abraham and
noted his lack of initiative and autonomy in his dealings with both
God and Sarah his wife (see Chapter 3). We also commented on
'another' Abraham that lurks in the shadows of the Genesis narrative – one that is assertive and who challenges divine justice. The
scene described in Genesis 18 offers another example of a paradigm
for being human against the grain of the dominant expectation.
Abraham normally plays out the role that Eve would not: he is
obedient to God to an extent that overrides his own interests, even
in terms of his paternal responsibilities and emotions. Yet, in the
account of God's judgement of Sodom, Abraham dares to question
the mind of God and, what is more, succeeds in changing God's
mind and deflecting, or at least delaying, the destruction of the city.
In Chapter 3 we noted the comment made by Danna Nolan Fewell
and David Gunn that it is disconcerting to discover that Abraham
would stand up to God for the sake of a city that had attracted the
wrath of God for good reason, and yet remain silent when God
commands him to slaughter his beloved son (see pp. 55).

It is even more surprising when the text includes an aside in
which God speculates on whether to disclose his decision to destroy
Sodom to Abraham, since he is one who 'does' righteousness and
justice (לעשות צדקה ומשפט) (Gen. 18.19). This insight into divine
thinking implies that God anticipates that Abraham would challenge the decision to slaughter all the inhabitants – guilty and
innocent alike. On this occasion the 'adult' Abraham exercises his
own judgement in deciding to challenge a theodicy that he believes
is neither right nor just. In the light of the subsequent narrative,
with the divine command to sacrifice Isaac, Abraham's words to God
here resound with irony:

> Far be it from you to do such a thing, to slay the righteous
> with the wicked, so that the righteous fare as the wicked!
> Far be that from you! Shall not the Judge of all the earth
> do what is just?
>
> (Gen. 18.25)

The utter depravity of the inhabitants of Sodom is revealed in the
next chapter when all the men of the city attempt to gang rape two
guests (described in the narrative as 'angels' (מלאכים) (Gen. 19.1))

who come to visit Lot, Abraham's uncle. The subsequent destruction of Sodom and the neighbouring town, Gomorrah, with sulphur and fire raining down from heaven, is not a total annulment of God's apparent change of heart during the earlier exchange with Abraham. The righteous are spared since Lot and his family are given the opportunity to escape – all except Lot's wife whose curiosity tempts her to disobey the instruction not to look back at the scene of destruction, with the result that she is turned into a pillar of salt. The conversation between God and Abraham in Genesis 18 allows the reader to glimpse an alternative, active role for Abraham in the divine plan, and to encounter a God who apparently suspends his omniscience to allow human judgement to prevail. In this scheme human autonomy is possible, and the words of the serpent are allowed to make sense: 'You will be like God, knowing good and evil' (Gen. 3.5).

In order to highlight the significance of this dialogue between God and Abraham, we should take a brief sideways glance at the book of Job, where there is a clear antithesis to it in terms of the human subject and the character of God. The main character, Job, questions the theodicy that allows him to be subjected to the most extreme pain and misfortune, despite his constant God-fearing innocence. The audience for the book of Job is provided at the beginning with an insight into the divine court, and this, to some degree, is intended to explain Job's predicament. This explanation, however, remains hidden from the subject throughout the book. Furthermore, since Job's suffering results simply from a wager between God and Satan, it is far from intellectually satisfying. Job's desperate plea for some clue as to why he is suffering is eventually answered directly by God. The answer comes in the form of a detailed statement outlining the totality of divine omnipotence and omniscience, and, as such, it stands to condemn Job for even daring to question divine justice. In the light of this revelation Job offers the appropriate response to the divine: 'I know that you can do all things, and that no purpose of yours can be thwarted' (42.1). There is no room for bargaining in this encounter with God.

The story of the Samaritan woman we discussed in Chapter 5 includes a dialogue that allows for the full engagement of human and divine agency. At the outset of the account the woman presents a mimesis of outcast womanhood – appearing at the well when no one is usually there. But this illusion of a 'non-person' evaporates in the light of the very different form of woman that emerges from this figure as the account unfolds. Unlike the disciples, she is presented as theologically informed, and she is confident to challenge the statements made by Jesus, prompting him eventually to reveal his messianic identity. When Jesus confronts her about her unconventional past and her marital status, she is unabashed and sees beyond her personal situation to the significance indicated by Jesus' power of insight. This woman is a true daughter of her inquiring and adventurous mother Eve, presenting humanity in full stature in the presence of God incarnate.

Constructed gender roles are consistently undermined in biblical narratives by characters who 'put on' and 'put off' gendered appearance and behaviour. For Tamar, Ruth and Judith femininity is something that is assumed. It is a guise performed in order to gain a specific end through acts of seduction, and these acts paradoxically expose both the hypocrisy of patriarchal systems and the vulnerability of masculinity. These strategies of 'gender-bending' are always set within the wider framework of expressing the inevitable outcome of the divine plan, but nevertheless they work to expose the fragility of polarised gender roles. They show that femininity is not something inscribed through biological essentialism – Judith can wear the guise of arch seductress as readily as she can play the part of the victorious warrior. These strategies signify the omnipotence of the divine and, at the same time, subvert the expectations for gendered behaviour. In doing so, they present vivid illustrations of performative gender theory, articulated by Judith Butler:

> That gender reality is created through sustained social performances means that the very notions of an essential sex and a true and abiding masculinity or femininity are also constituted as part of a strategy that conceals gender's performative character and the performative possibilities for proliferating gender configurations outside the restricting frames of masculinist domination and compulsory heterosexuality.
>
> (1990: 141)

The boundaries that are broken by divine performance on the biblical stage often involve the suspension of the given, normative, human behavioural patterns. As we have noted in previous chapters, from the viewpoint of modernity, the patterns that suspend human maturity are difficult to assimilate with our expectations of autonomy, for example the prelapsarian Adam and Eve, Abraham in terms of his family situation, and the children of God shaped by the apostle Paul. However, this suspension of the norm in relation to gendered behaviour offers paradigms for human identity that resonate with postmodern experience, going beyond static masculine and feminine polarised duality. In this sense biblical texts can offer radical illustrations of ways of being human that challenge societal norms – both in terms of behaviour and sexual identity. Biblical discourses can subvert as well as uphold normative power paradigms and, in doing, so demonstrate Foucault's theory of the genealogy of power: 'Discourse transmits and produces power; it reinforces it, but also undermines and exposes it, renders it fragile and makes it possible to thwart it' (1984: 100).

In previous chapters we have exposed an anarchic theme that runs through biblical literature, where laws are broken and expectations shattered, and which can stand as a challenge to humanity to question the given socio-political structures, and to deconstruct normative patterns for behaviour. The Bible offers us a deity that defies convention, as it overrides custom and law to fulfil the divine plan. Within biblical discourse it is always the omniscience and omnipotence of God that is both demonstrated and served by the suspension of human or natural law. From the human perspective there remains a blueprint for those who would be unconventional and who would question societies that demand conformity in terms of identity and behaviour. The biblical God does not need to be diluted to fit the liberal patriarch we have tended to meet in commentaries written since the rise of historical criticism, or to be squeezed into a tiny depatriarchalised mould feminist scholars have prepared, or even to be modified to become the champion of the dispossessed. The biblical deity can be all these things, as well as being the God who slays the enemies of Israel, and who can demand child-sacrifice from Abraham, kill the innocent Job's wife and children as part of a wager, encourage Rebecca to deceive her husband, and deny the rights of her eldest son. God's love is undeniably attested to throughout the Bible, but the character of that love is contingent upon the meaning, and limitations, of the metaphors and imagery drawn on by the biblical authors in their times. The concept of paternal love in the context of the Roman Empire is inevitably and inextricably bound up with absolute authority and power. 'Fatherhood' as understood in the first century can demand the exposure of newborn babies or the brutal massacre of children in the arena. In translating this metaphor uncritically to our own time, levels of meaning intrinsic to the metaphor in its biblical context are neither confronted nor challenged.

If the meaning of 'fatherhood' is developed in the light of its context in biblical times, by allowing scholars of antiquity to add their insights to the work of contemporary theologians and philosophers of religion, then new language for human experience of the divine might gain added conviction. The concept of divine love that the biblical reader today identifies with from their own experience – spiritually and materially – will be, as ever, a concept that resonates with their own situation.

Reflecting on the hermeneutical approach suggested by the Asian post-colonial theologian Kwok Pui-lan, Fernando Segovia observes radical shifts away from traditional claims about the Bible:

> Sacrality – the Bible not as the sacred text of God but as a human construction of the sacred among others, subject to testing and reappropriation in other cultural contexts; canonicity – the Bible not as the closed collection of God's truth but as a collection signifying both the inclusion and the repression of truth, subject to expansion by way of other cultural traditions and religions; normativity – the Bible not as the locus of God's presence but as a 'talking-Book', subject to multiple interpretations and evaluations in multiple cultural contexts.
>
> (2000: 76–7)

For readers and hearers of the Bible in the twenty-first century, who live in the paradox of globalisation and fragmentation, the discontinuities of the Bible that are manifest under the shade of abiding omnipotence make a different sort of sense than the ironed-out biblical theologies, or salvation histories, offered by previous generations. Those who can welcome the Bible's *dis*continuities can marvel at the moral spectrum presented by the many and varied representations of God in biblical literature, and as part of a humanity that has come of age – that has eaten of the tree of knowledge – can judge and discern which god is their God through their own imaginations and their own moral categories. Taking this stance an individual or a community does not shrink from rejecting texts that are relatively immoral, or from re-evaluating those that resonate with our own contexts, in a process that is liberating for both the text and the reader.

BIBLIOGRAPHY

Aberbach, D. (1993) *Imperialism and Biblical Prophecy 750–500 BCE*, London: Routledge.

Adler, R. (1977) 'A Mother in Israel: Aspects of the Mother Role in Jewish Myth', in R. M. Gross (ed.) *Beyond Androcentrism – New Essays on Women and Religion*, Missoula, MT: Scholars Press, pp. 237–55.

Aichele, G. (2001) *The Control of Biblical Meaning: Canon as Semiotic Mechanism*, Harrisburg, PA: Trinity Press International.

Aichele, G., Burnett, F. W. and Castelli, E. A. *et al.* (1995) *The Postmodern Bible*, New Haven, CT: Yale University Press.

Albertz, R. (1994) *A History of Israelite Religion in the Old Testament Period, Vol. 1: From the Beginnings to the End of the Exile, Vol. 2: From the Exile to the Maccabees*, London: SCM Press; Louisville, KY: Westminster/John Knox.

Albright, W. F. (1920) 'The Goddess of Life and Wisdom', *American Journal of Semitic Languages* 36: 258–94.

Alonso-Schokel, L. (1975) 'Narrative Structures in the Book of Judith', in W. Wuellner (ed.) *Protocol Series of the Colloquies of the Center for Hermeneutical Studies in Hellenistic and Modern Culture*, Vol. 11, No. 17, Berkeley: University of California, pp.1–20.

Alter, R. (1981) *The Art of Biblical Narrative*, New York: Basic Books.

Alter, R. (1983) 'From Line to Story in Biblical Verse', *Poetics Today* 4: 615–37.

Alter, R. (1996) *Genesis: Translation and Commentary*, New York and London: W. W. Norton.

Alter, R. and Kermode, F. (eds) (1987) *The Literary Guide to the Bible*, Cambridge, MA: Harvard University Press.

Armour, E. T. (1999) *Deconstruction, Feminist Theology, and the Problem of Difference: Subverting the Race/Gender Divide*, Chicago: University of Chicago Press.

Augustine of Hippo (1982) *The Literal Meaning of Genesis*, trans. J. Taylor and S. J. Hammond, New York: Newman Press.

Baer, R. A. (1970) *Philo's Use of the Categories Male and Female*, Leiden: E. J. Brill.

Bakhtin, M. (1981) *The Dialogic Imagination: Four Essays*, trans. C. Emerson and M. Holquist, Austin: University of Texas Press.

Bal, M. (1987) *Lethal Love: Feminist Biblical Readings of Biblical Love Stories*, Bloomington: Indiana University Press.

Bal, M. (1988a) *Murder and Difference: Genre, Gender and Scholarship on Sisera's Death*, Bloomington: Indiana University Press.

Bal, M. (1988b) *Death and Dissymmetry: The Politics of Coherence in the Book of Judges*, Chicago: University of Chicago Press.

Bal, M. (1990) 'Dealing/With/Women: Daughters in the Book of Judges', in R. M. Schwartz (ed.) *The Book and the Text: The Bible and Literary Theory*, Cambridge: Blackwell, pp. 16–39.

Balsdon, J. P. V. D. (1962) *Roman Women: Their History and Habits*, London: The Bodley Head.

Barth, K. (1956) *Church Dogmatics, IV.1*, Edinburgh: T. & T. Clark.

Barton, M. (1999) *Scripture as Empowerment for Liberation and Justice: The Experience of Christian and Muslim Women in Bangladesh*, Centre for Comparative Studies in Religion and Gender Monograph Series 1, Bristol: CCSRG.

Beal, T. K. (1997) *The Book of Hiding: Gender, Ethnicity, Annihilation, and Esther*, London: Routledge.

Beal, T. K. and Gunn, D. M. (eds) (1997) *Reading Bibles, Writing Bodies: Identity and The Book*, London: Routledge.

Beal, T. K. and Gunn, D. M. (1999) 'Judges, Book of', in J. H. Hayes (ed.) *Dictionary of Biblical Interpretation*, Nashville, TN: Abingdon, pp. 637–47.

Beard, M. (1994) 'The Roman and the Foreign: The Cult of the "Great Mother" in Imperial Rome', in N. Thomas and C. Humphrey (eds) *Shamanism, History and the State*, Michigan: University of Michigan Press, pp. 164–90.

Beard, M. and Henderson, J. (1998) 'With This Body I Thee Worship: Sacred Prostitution in Antiquity', in M. Wyke (ed.) *Gender and the Body in the Ancient Mediterranean*, Oxford: Blackwell, pp. 56–79.

Beard, M., North, J. and Price, S. (1998) *Religions of Rome, Vol. 1: A History*, Cambridge: Cambridge University Press.

Beauvoir, S. de (1970) *The Second Sex*, trans. H. M. Parshley, New York: Knopf.

Berlant, L. (1997) *The Queen of America Goes to Washington City: Essays on Sex and Citizenship*, Durham: Duke University Press.

Bigger, S. (1979) 'The Family Laws of Leviticus 18 in Their Setting', *Journal of Biblical Literature* 98: 187–203.

Bird, P. (1989) 'The Harlot as Heroine: Narrative Art and Social Presupposition in Three Old Testament Texts', *Semeia* 46: 119–39.

Boling, R. G. (1975) *Judges: A New Translation with Introduction and Commentary*, The Anchor Bible series, Garden City, NY: Doubleday and Co.

Bos, J. W. H. (1988) 'Out of the Shadows: Genesis 38; Judges 4:17–22; Ruth 3', in C. J. Exum and J W. H. Bos (eds), 'Reasoning with the Foxes: Female Wit in a World of Male Power', *Semeia* 42 pp. 37–67.

Boyarin, D. (1994) *A Radical Jew: Paul and the Politics of Identity*, Berkeley: University of California Press.

Boyarin, D. (1995) 'Are There Any Jews in "The History of Sexuality"?', *Journal of the History of Sexuality* 3: 333–55.

Boyarin, D. (1999) *Dying For God: Martyrdom and the Making of Christianity and Judaism*, Stanford, CA: Stanford University Press.

Brenner, A. (1993) 'Naomi and Ruth', in A. Brenner (ed.) *A Feminist Companion to Ruth*, Sheffield: Sheffield Academic Press, pp. 70–84.

Brenner, A. (1994) 'An Afterword: The Decalogue – Am I the Addressee?', in A. Brenner (ed.) *A Feminist Companion to Exodus-Deuteronomy*, Sheffield: Sheffield Academic Press, pp. 255–8.

Brenner, A. (ed.) (1998) *Genesis: A Feminist Companion to the Bible*, Second Series, Sheffield: Sheffield Academic Press.

Brenner, A. (ed.) (1999) *Judges: A Feminist Companion to the Bible*, Second Series, Sheffield: Sheffield Academic Press.

Brenner, A. and Fontaine, C. (eds) (1997) *A Feminist Companion to Reading the Bible: Approaches, Methods and Strategies*, Sheffield: Sheffield Academic Press.

Brenner, A. and van Dijk-Hemmes, F. (1993) *On Gendering Texts: Female and Male Voices in the Hebrew Bible*, Leiden: Brill.

Brett, M. (2000) *Genesis: Procreation and the Politics of Identity*, London: Routledge.

Briggs, S. (1995) 'Galatians', in E. Schüssler Fiorenza (ed.) *Searching the Scriptures, Vol. 2: A Commentary*, New York: Crossroad, pp. 218–36.

Brooten, B. J. (1985) 'Early Christian Women and Their Cultural Context: Issues of Method in Historical Reconstruction', in A. Y. Collins (ed.) *Feminist Perspectives on Biblical Scholarship*, Chico, CA: Scholars Press.

Brooten, B. J. (1996) *Love Between Women: Early Christian Responses to Female Homoeroticism*, Chicago: University of Chicago Press.

Brueggemann, W. (1992) *Old Testament Theology: Essays on Structure, Theme, and Text*, Patrick D. Miller (ed.), Minneapolis, MN: Fortress Press.

Brueggemann, W. (1997) *Theology of the Old Testament: Testimony, Dispute, Advocacy*, Minneapolis, MN: Fortress Press.

Burrus, V. (2000) *Begotten, Not Made: Conceiving Manhood in Late Antiquity*, Stanford, CA: Stanford University Press.

Butler, J. (1990) *Gender Trouble: Feminism and the Subversion of Identity*, London: Routledge.

Butler, J. (1993) *Bodies That Matter: On the Discursive Limits of 'Sex'*, London: Routledge.

Butler, J. (1997) *The Psychic Life of Power: Theories in Subjection*, Stanford, CA: Stanford University Press.

Camp, C. V. (1985) *Wisdom and the Feminine in the Book of Proverbs*, Sheffield: Sheffield Academic Press.

Camp, C. V. (1997) 'Woman Wisdom and the Strange Woman: Where is Power to be Found?' in T. K. Beal and D. M. Gunn (eds) *Reading Bibles, Writing Bodies: Identity and The Book*, London: Routledge.

Camp, C. V. (2000) *Wise, Strange and Holy: The Strange Woman and the Making of the Bible*, Sheffield: Sheffield Academic Press.

Carmichael, C. (1974) *The Laws of Deuteronomy*, Ithaca, NY: Cornell University Press.

Carroll, R. C. (1986) *Jeremiah: A Commentary*, London: SCM Press.

Castelli, E. A. (1991) *Imitating Paul: A Discourse of Power*, Louisville, KY: Westminster.

Chopp, R. S. and Davaney, S. G. (eds) (1997) *Horizons in Feminist Theology: Identity, Tradition, and Norms*, Minneapolis, MN: Fortress Press.

Clark, E. A. (1984) *Women in the Early Church*, Lewiston, NY: Edwin Mellen.

Clark, E. A. (1995) 'Antifamilial Tendencies in Ancient Christianity', *Journal of the History of* Sexuality 5(3): 356–80.

Clark, E. A. (1999) *Reading Renunciation: Asceticism and Scripture in Early Christianity*, Princeton, NJ: Princeton University Press.

Clifford, G. (1973) *The Interpretation of Cultures*, New York: Basic Books.

Clines, D. J. A. (1990) *What Does Eve Do to Help? And Other Readerly Questions to the Old Testament*, Sheffield: Sheffield Academic Press.

Clines, D. J. A. (1997) *The Theme of the Pentateuch*, 2nd edition, Sheffield: Sheffield Academic Press.

Collins, A. Y. (ed.) (1985) *Feminist Perspectives on Biblical Scholarship*, Chico, CA: Scholars Press.

Collins, J. J. and Sterling, G. E. (eds) (2001) *Hellenism in the Land of Israel*, Notre Dame, IN: University of Notre Dame Press.

Collins, R. (1995) 'From John to the Beloved Disciple: An Essay on Johannine Characters', *Interpretation* 49: 359–69.

Conway, C. M. (1999) *Men and Women in the Fourth Gospel: Gender and Johannine Characterization*, SBL Dissertation Series 167, Atlanta, GA: Society of Biblical Literature.

Corbier, M. (2001) 'Child Exposure and Abandonment', in S. Dixon (ed.) *Childhood, Class and Kin in the Roman World*, London: Routledge, pp. 52–73.

Craven, T. (1983) *Artistry and Faith in the Book of Judith*, Chico, CA: Scholars Press.

Crook, J. A. (1967) 'Patria Potestas', *Classical Quarterly* 17: 113–22.

Daly, M. (1973) *Beyond God the Father: Toward a Philosophy of Women's Liberation*, Boston, MA: Beacon Press.

D'Angelo, M. R. (1992) '*Abba* and "Father": Imperial Theology and the Jesus Traditions', *Journal of Biblical Literature* 111(4): 611–30.

D'Angelo, M. R. (1999) '(Re)Presentations of Women in the Gospels: John and Mark', in R. Shepard Kraemer and M. R. D'Angelo (eds) *Women and Christian Origins*, Oxford: Oxford University Press, pp. 129–49.

Darr, K. Pfisterer (1994) *Isaiah's Vision and the Family of God*, Louisville, KY: Westminster/John Knox Press.

Delaney, C. (1998) 'Abraham and the Seeds of Patriarchy', in A. Brenner (ed.) *Genesis: A Feminist Companion to the Bible*, Second Series, Sheffield: Sheffield Academic Press, pp. 129–49.

Derrida, J. (1981a) *Positions*, trans. A. Bass, Chicago: University of Chicago Press.

Derrida, J. (1981b) 'Plato's Pharmacy', in *Dissemination*, London: Athlone Press.

Dewey, J. (1995) 'The Gospel of Mark', in E. Schüssler Fiorenza (ed.) *Searching the Scriptures, Vol 2: A Commentary*, New York: Crossroad, pp. 470–509.

Dixon, S. (1988) *The Roman Mother*, London: Croom Helm.

BIBLIOGRAPHY

Dixon, S. (1991) 'The Sentimental Ideal of the Roman Family', in B. Rawson (ed.) *Marriage, Divorce and Children in Ancient Rome*, Canberra/Oxford: Clarendon Press, pp. 99–113.

Dixon, S. (2001a) *Reading Roman Women*, London: Duckworth.

Dixon, S. (ed.) (2001b) *Childhood, Class and Kin in the Roman World*, London: Routledge.

Douglas, M. (1999) *Leviticus As Literature*, Oxford: Oxford University Press.

Duke, P. D. (1985) *Irony in the Fourth Gospel*, Atlanta,GA: John Knox Press.

Eilberg-Schwartz, H. (1990) *The Savage in Judaism: An Anthropology of Israelite Religion and Ancient Judaism*, Bloomington: Indiana University Press.

Eissfeldt, O. (1965) *The Old Testament: An Introduction. The History of the Formation of the Old Testament*, Oxford: Blackwell.

Elder, L. B. (1995) 'Judith', in E. Schüssler Fiorenza (ed.) *Searching the Scriptures, Vol. 2: A Commentary*, New York: Crossroad, pp. 455–69.

Eslinger, L. (1987) 'The Wooing of the Woman at the Well: Jesus, The Reader and Reader-Response Criticism', *Journal of Literature and Theology* 1: 167–83.

Exum, J. C. (1996) *Plotted, Shot, and Painted: Cultural Representations of Biblical Women*, Sheffield: Sheffield Academic Press.

Fantham, E. *et al.*, (1994) *Women in the Classical World*, Oxford: Oxford University Press.

Fewell, D. Nolan (1992) 'Judges', in C. A. Newsom and S. H. Ringe (eds) *The Women's Bible Commentary*, London and Louisville, KY: SPCK and Westminster/John Knox Press.

Fewell, D. Nolan (1997) 'Imagination, Method and Murder: Un/framing the Face of Post-Exilic Israel', in T. K. Beal and D M. Gunn (eds) *Reading Bibles, Writing Bodies: Identity and The Book*, London: Routledge.

Fewell, D. Nolan and Gunn, D. M. (1988) 'A Son is Born to Naomi: Literary Allusions and Interpretation in the Book of Ruth', *Journal for the Study of the Old Testament* 40: 99–108.

Fewell, D. Nolan and Gunn, D. M. (1993) *Gender, Power and Promise: The Subject of the Bible's First Story*, Nashville, TN: Abingdon Press.

Fiorenza, E. Schüssler (1984) *Bread Not Stone: The Challenge of Feminist Biblical Interpretation*, Boston, MA: Beacon Press.

Fiorenza, E. Schüssler (ed.) (1994/1995a) *Searching the Scriptures, Vol. 1: A Feminist Introduction, Vol. 2: A Commentary*, London: SCM Press.

Fiorenza, E. Schüssler (1995b) *In Memory of Her: A Feminist Theological Reconstruction of Christian Origins*, 2nd edition, London: SCM Press.

Firestone, S. (1979) *The Dialectic of Sex: The Case for Feminist Revolution*, new edition, London: Women's Press.

Foucault, M. (1984) *The History of Sexuality: An Introduction*, London: Penguin Books.

Foucault, M. (1988) *The Care of the Self: History of Sexuality Vol. 3*, London: Penguin Books.

Foxhall, L. and Salmon, J. (eds) (1998) *When Men Were Men: Masculinity, Power and Identity in Classical Antiquity*, London: Routledge.

Fradenburg, L. and Freccero, C. (eds) (1996) *Premodern Sexualities*, London: Routledge.

Freedman, D. N. (1976) 'Deuteronomic History, The' in K. Crim (ed.) *The Interpreters' Dictionary of the Bible, Supplementary Volume*, Nashville, TN: Abingdon, pp. 226–8.

Fuchs, E. (1982) 'Status and Role of Female Heroines in the Biblical Narrative', *Mankind Quarterly* 23: 149–60.

Fuchs, E. (1985) 'Who is Hiding the Truth? Deceptive Women and Biblical Androcentrism', in A. Y. Collins (ed.) *Feminist Perspectives on Biblical Scholarship*, Chico, CA: Scholars Press, pp. 137–44.

Fulkerson, M. M. (1994) *Changing the Subject: Women's Discourses and Feminist Theology*, Minneapolis, MN: Fortress Press.

Gardner, H. (ed.) (1972) *Oxford Book of English Verse 1250–1950*, Oxford: Oxford University Press.

Gaventa, B. (1990) 'The Maternity of Paul: An Exegetical Study of Galatians 4.19', in R. Fortna and B. Gaventa (eds) *The Conversation Continues: Studies in Paul and John in Honor of J. Louis Martyn*, Nashville, TN: Abingdon Press, pp. 189–210.

Geertz, C. (1973) *The Interpretation of Cultures*, New York: Basic Books.

Gilhus, I. S. (1983) 'Male and Female Symbolism in the Gnostic Apocryphon of John', *Temenos* 19: 33–43.

Gössmann, E. (1999) 'The Image of God and the Human Being in Women's Counter-Tradition', in D. F. Sawyer and D. M. Collier (eds) *Is There A Future for Feminist Theology?*, Sheffield: Sheffield Academic Press, pp. 26–56.

Grant, J. (1989) *White Women's Christ and Black Women's Jesus*, Atlanta, GA: Scholars Press.

Greer, G. (1981) *The Obstacle Race: The Fortunes of Women Painters and Their Work*, London: Pan Books.

Gunn, D. M. (2000) 'Hebrew Narrative', in A. D. H. Mayes (ed.) *Text in Context: Essays by Members of the Society for Old Testament Study*, Oxford: Oxford University Press.

Gunn, D. M. and Fewell, D. Nolan (1993) *Narrative in the Hebrew Bible*, Oxford Bible Series, Oxford: Oxford University Press.

Halperin, D. M., Winkler, J. J. and Zeitlin, F. I. (eds) (1990) *Before Sexuality: The Construction of Erotic Experience in the Ancient Greek World*, Princeton, NJ: Princeton University Press.

Hawley, R. and Levick, B. (eds) (1995) *Women in Antiquity: New Assessments*, London: Routledge.

Henten, J. W. van (1995) 'Judith as Alternative Leader: A Rereading of Judith 7–13', in A. Brenner (ed.) *A Feminist Companion to Esther, Judith and Susanna*, Sheffield: Sheffield Academic Press, pp. 224–52.

Holladay, W. L. (1966) 'Jer. XXXI 22b Reconsidered: "The Woman Encompasses the Man"', *Vetus Testamentum* 16: 236–9.

Holladay, W. L. (1989) *Jeremiah 2: A Commentary on the Book of the Prophet Jeremiah Chapters 26–52*, Minneapolis, MN: Fortress Press.

Irigaray, L. (1985) *This Sex Which Is Not One*, trans. C. Porter with C. Burke, Ithaca, NY: Cornell University Press.

Irigaray, L. (1991) *Marine Lover of Friedrich Nietzsche*, trans. G. C. Gill, New York: Columbia University Press.

Kahl, B. (1999) 'Gender trouble in Galatia? Paul and the Rethinking of Difference', in D. F. Sawyer and D. M. Collier (eds) *Is There A Future for Feminist Theology?*, Sheffield: Sheffield Academic Press, pp. 57–73.

Keith, A. M. (2000) *Engendering Rome: Women in Latin Epic*, Cambridge: Cambridge University Press.

Klein, C. (1975) *Anti-Judaism in Christian Theology*, Philadelphia, PA: Fortress Press.

Köves-Zulaf, T. (1990) *Römische Geburtsriten*, Munich: Beck.

Kraemer, R. Shepard (1992) *Her Share of the Blessings: Women's Religions Among Pagans, Jews, and Christians in the Greco-Roman World*, Oxford: Oxford University Press.

Kraemer, R. Shepard and D'Angelo M. R. (eds) (1999) *Women and Christian Origins*, Oxford: Oxford University Press.

Kramer, P. Silverman (1998) 'Biblical Women that Come in Pairs: The Use of Female Pairs as a Literary Device in the Hebrew Bible', in A. Brenner (ed.) *Genesis: A Feminist Companion to the Bible*, Second Series, Sheffield: Sheffield Academic Press, pp. 218–32.

Lacan, J. (1977) 'The Mirror Stage as Formative of the Function of the I as Revealed in Psychoanalytical Experience', in *Ecrits: A Selection*, trans. A. Sheridan London: Tavistock, pp. 1–7.

LaCocque, A. (1990) *The Feminine Unconventional: Four Subversive Figures in Israel's Tradition*, Minneapolis, MN: Fortress Press.

LaCocque, A. and Ricoeur, P. (1998) *Thinking Biblically: Exegetical and Hermeneutical Studies*, trans. D. Pellauer, Chicago: Chicago University Press.

Landy, F. (1997) 'Do We Want Our Children to Read This Book?' in D. Nolan Fewell and G. A. Phillips (eds) 'Bible and Ethics of Reading', *Semeia* 77, pp. 157–76.

Lassen, E. M. (1997) 'The Roman Family: Ideal and Metaphor', in H. Moxnes (ed.) *Constructing Early Christian Families: Family as Social Reality and Metaphor*, London: Routledge, pp. 103–20.

Lee, D. A. (1999) 'The Symbol of Divine Fatherhood', in A. Reinhartz (ed.) 'God the Father in the Gospel of John', *Semeia* 85, Atlanta, Georgia: Society of Biblical Literature, pp. 177–87.

Lemche, N. P. (1993) 'The Old Testament – A Hellenistic Book?', *Journal for the Study of the Old Testament* 7: 163–93.

Levine, Amy-Jill (1995) 'Sacrifice and Salvation: Otherness and Domestication in the Book of Judith', in Athalya Brenner (ed.), *A Feminist Companion to Esther, Judith and Susanna*, Sheffield: Sheffield Academic Press, pp. 208–23.

Lieu, Judith (1996) *Image and Reality: The Jews in the World of the Christians in the Second Century*, Edinburgh: T. & T. Clark.

Margalit, B. (1990) 'The Meaning and Significance of Asherah', *Vetus Testamentum* 40: 264–97.

Marshall, I. H. (1974) 'The Problem of New Testament Exegesis', *Journal of the Evangelical Theology Society* 17.

Martin, D. B. (1995) *The Corinthian Body*, New Haven, CT: Yale University Press.

Martin, D. B. (1997) 'Paul without Passion: On Paul's Rejection of Desire in Sex and Marriage' in H. Moxnes (ed.) *Constructing Early Christian Families: Family as Social Reality and Metaphor*, London: Routledge, pp. 201–15.

Martin, R. P. (1972) *Mark – Evangelist and Theologian*, Exeter: Paternoster Press.

Mayes, A. D. H. (ed.) (2000) *Text in Context: Essays by Members of the Society for Old Testament Study*, Oxford: Oxford University Press.

McFague, S. (1982) *Metaphorical Theology: Models of God in Religious Language*, London: SCM Press.

McKane, W. (1970) *Proverbs: A New Approach*, Philadelphia, PA: Westminster.

McKane, W. (1996) *A Critical and Exegetical Commentary on Jeremiah, Vol. II*, Edinburgh: T. & T. Clark.

McKinlay, J. E. (1996) *Gendering the Host: Biblical Invitations to Eat and Drink*, Sheffield: Sheffield Academic Press.

Meeks, W. (1974) 'The Image of the Androgyne: Some Uses of a Symbol in Earliest Christianity', *History of Religions* 13: 165–208.

Milgrom, J. (1993) 'Leviticus' in W. Meeks (ed.) *The HarperCollins Study Bible*, pp. 151–97.

Moi, T. (1985) *Sexual/Textual Politics: Feminist Literary Theory*, London: Methuen.

Montley, P. (1978) 'Judith in the Fine Arts: The Appeal of the Archetypal Androgyne', *Anima* 4: 37–42.

Moore, C. A. (1985) *Judith*, Garden City, New York: Doubleday.

Moore, G. Foot (1927; reprinted1971) *Judaism in the First Centuries of the Christian Era*, New York: Schocken.

Moore, S. (1996) *God's Gym: Divine Male Bodies of the Bible*, London: Routledge.

Morris, P. and Sawyer, D. F. (eds) (1992) *A Walk in the Garden: Biblical, Iconographical and Literary Images of Eden*, Sheffield: Sheffield Academic Press.

Moxnes, H. (ed.) (1997) *Constructing Early Christian Families: Family as Social Reality and Metaphor*, London: Routledge.

Musurillo, H. (1972) *The Acts of the Christian Martyrs: Introduction, Texts and Translations*, Oxford: Oxford University Press.

Niditch, S. (1979) 'The Wronged Woman Righted: An Analysis of Genesis 38', *Harvard Theological Review* 72: 143–9.

Niditch, S. (1982) 'The "Sodomite" Theme in Judges 19–20: Family, Community and Social Disintegration', *Catholic Bible Quarterly* 44: 365–78.

O'Day, G. R. (1986) *Revelation in the Fourth Gospel*, Philadelphia: Fortress Press.

O'Day, G. R. (1992) 'John', in C. A. Newsom and S. H. Ringe (eds) *The Women's Bible Commentary*, London and Louisville, KY: SPCK and Westminster/John Knox Press, pp. 293–304.

Olyan, S. M. (1988) *Asherah and the Cult of Yahweh in Israel*, Atlanta, GA: Scholars Press.

Olyan, S. M. (1994) '"And With a Male You Shall Not Lie the Lying Down of a Woman": On the Meaning and Significance of Leviticus 18.22 and 20.13', *Journal of the History of Sexuality* 5(2): 179–206.

Orsiek, C. (1992) 'Galatians', in C. A. Newsom and S. H. Ringe (eds) *The Women's Bible Commentary*, London and Louisville, KY: SPCK and Westminster/John Knox Press, pp. 333–7.

Ostriker, A. S. (1994) *The Nakedness of the Fathers: Biblical Visions and Revisions*, New Brunswick, NJ: Rutgers University Press.

Parker, I. K. (1999) 'Mirror, Mirror on the Wall, Must We Leave Eden, Once and for All? A Lacanian Pleasure Trip Through the Garden', *Journal for the Study of the Old Testament* 83: 3–17.

Parkin, T. (2001) 'On Becoming a Parent in Later Life: from Augustus to Antonio Agustín via St Augustine', in S. Dixon (ed.) *Childhood, Class and Kin in the Roman World*, London: Routledge, pp. 221–34.

Pazdan, M. M. (1987) 'Nicodemus and the Samaritan Woman: Contrasting Models of Discipleship', *Biblical Theological Bulletin* 17: 145–8.

Peterson, E. (1959) 'Einige Bemerkungen zum Hamburger Papyrus', in *Frühkirche, Judentum und Gnosis*, Rome/Freiburg/Vienna: Herder pp. 194–6.

Piskorowski, A. (1992) 'In Search of Her Father: A Lacanian Approach to Genesis 2–3', in P. Morris and D. F. Sawyer (eds) *A Walk in the Garden: Biblical, Iconographical and Literary Images of Eden*, Sheffield: Sheffield Academic Press, pp. 310–18.

Plaskow, J. (1978) 'Christian Feminism and Anti-Judaism', *Cross-Currents* 33: 306–9.

Plaskow, J. (1994) 'Anti-Judaism in Feminist Christian Interpretation', in E. Schüssler Fiorenza (ed.) *Searching the Scriptures, Vol. 1: A Feminist Introduction*, London: SCM Press, pp. 117–29.

Polaski, S. H. (1999) *Paul and the Discourse of Power*, Sheffield: Sheffield Academic Press.

Rad, G. von (1972a) *Wisdom in Israel*, trans. J. D. Martin, Nashville, TN: Abingdon.

Rad, G. von (1972b) *Genesis: A Commentary*, Old Testament Library, trans. J. H. Marks, revised edition, Philadelphia, PA: Westminster.

Rashkow, I. N. (2000) *Taboo or Not Taboo: Sexuality and Family in the Hebrew Bible*, Minneapolis, MN: Fortress Press.

Rawson, B. (1992) 'Children in the Roman *Familia*', in B. Rawson (ed.) *The Family in Ancient Rome*, London: Routledge, pp. 170–200.

Reinhartz, A. (1995) 'The Gospel of John', in E. Schüssler Fiorenza (ed.) *Searching the Scriptures, Vol. 2: A Commentary*, New York: Crossroad, pp. 561–600.

Reinhartz, A. (ed.) (1999) 'God the Father in the Gospel of John', *Semeia* 85, Atlanta, GA: Society of Biblical Literature.

Ricoeur, P. (1974) 'Fatherhood: From Phantasm to Symbol', in *The Conflict of Interpretations: Paul Ricoeur Essays in Hermeneutics*, Evanston, IL: Northwestern University Press, pp. 468–97.

Roberts, R. H. (1992) 'Sin, Saga and Gender', in P. Morris and D. F. Sawyer (eds) *A Walk in the Garden: Biblical, Iconographical and Literary Images of Eden*, Sheffield: Sheffield Academic Press, pp. 244–60.

Rollins, W. G. (1999) *Soul and Psyche: The Bible in Psychological Perspective*, Minneapolis, MN: Fortress Press.

Rudman, D. (2001) 'Falling For the Wrong Woman? A Theological Reassessment of Genesis 2–3', *Expository Times* 113(2): 44–7.

Ruether, R. Radford (1985) *Womanguides: Readings Toward a Feminist Theology*, Boston, MA: Beacon Press.

Ruether, R. Radford (2000) *Christianity and the Making of the Modern Family*, Boston, MA: Beacon Press.

Salisbury, J. (1997) *Perpetua's Passion: The Death and Memory of a Young Roman Woman*, London: Routledge.

Sasson, J. M. (1989) *Ruth: A New Translation with a Philological Commentary and a Formalist–Folklorist Interpretation*, 2nd edition, Sheffield: Sheffield Academic Press.

Sawyer, D. F. (1992) ' Resurrecting Eve?', in P. Morris and D. F. Sawyer (eds) *A Walk in the Garden: Biblical, Iconographical and Literary Images of Eden*, Sheffield: Sheffield Academic Press, pp. 273–89.

Sawyer, D. F. (1996) *Women and Religion in the First Christian Centuries*, London: Routledge.

Sawyer, D. F. (1999) 'Gender-play and Sacred Text: A Scene From Jeremiah', *Journal for the Study of the Old Testament* 83: 99–111.

Sawyer, D. F. (2001a) 'Dressing Up/Dressing Down: Power, Performance and Identity in the Book of Judith', in *Theology and Sexuality*, 15: 23–31.

Sawyer, D. F. (2001b) 'Gender Strategies in Antiquity: Judith's Performance' *Feminist Theology* 28: 9–26.

Sawyer, D. F. (2001c) 'A Male Bible?', *Expository Times* 112(11): 366–9.

Sawyer, D. F. and Collier, D. M. (eds) (1999) *Is There A Future for Feminist Theology?*, Sheffield: Sheffield Academic Press.

Schor, N. and Weed, E. (eds) (1994) *The Essential Difference*, Bloomington and Indianapolis: Indiana University Press.

Schrenk, G. and Quell, G. (1967) 'πατηρ', in G. Friedrich (ed.) *Theological Dictionary of the New Testament, Vol. V*, Amsterdam: Eerdmans, pp. 945–1014.

Segovia, F. F. (2000) 'Reading Across: Intercultural Criticism and Textual Posture', in F. F. Segovia (ed.) *Interpreting Beyond Borders*, Sheffield: Sheffield Academic Press, pp 59–83.

Seters, J. van (1992) *Prologue to History*, Louisville, KY: Westminster/John Knox.

Sherwood, Y. (2000) *A Biblical Text and Its Afterlives: The Survival of Jonah in Western Culture*, Cambridge: Cambridge University Press.

Soggin, J. A. (1981) *Judges*, Old Testament Library, Philadelphia: Westminster Press.

Stocker, M. (1998) *Judith Sexual Warrior: Women and Power in Western Culture*, New Haven, CT and London: Yale University Press.

Stone, K. (1996) *Sex, Honor and Power in the Deuteronomistic History*, Sheffield: Sheffield Academic Press.

Streete, G. C. (1997) *The Strange Woman: Power and Sex in the Bible*, Louisville. KY: WJK.

Teubal, S. J. (1993) 'Sarah and Hagar: Matriarchs and Visionaries' in A. Brenner (ed.), *A Feminist Companion to Genesis*, Sheffield: Sheffield Academic Press, pp. 235–50.

Thompson, J. L. (2001) *Writing the Wrongs: Women of the Old Testament Among Biblical Commentators From Philo Through the Reformation*, Oxford: Oxford University Press.

Tolbert, M. A. (1992) 'Mark', in C. A. Newsom and S. H. Ringe (eds) *The Women's Bible Commentary*, London and Louisville, KY: SPCK and Westminster/John Knox Press, pp. 263–74.

Trible, P. (1973) 'Depatriarchalizing in the Biblical Tradition', *Journal of the American Academy of Religion* 41: 30–48.

Trible, P. (1978) *God and the Rhetoric of Sexuality*, Philadelphia, PA: Fortress Press.

Trible, P. (1984) *Texts of Terror: Literary Feminist Readings of Biblical Narratives*, Philadelphia: Fortress Press.

Urbach, E. E. (1987) *The Sages: The World and Wisdom of the Rabbis of the Talmud*, Cambridge, MA: Harvard University Press.

Uro, R. (1997) 'Asceticism and Anti-Familial Language in the *Gospel of Thomas*', in H. Moxnes (ed.) *Constructing Early Christian Families: Family as Social Reality and Metaphor*, London: Routledge, pp. 216–34.

Valler, S. (1999) 'The Story of Jephthah's Daughter in the Midrash', in A. Brenner (ed.) *Judges: A Feminist Companion to the Bible*, Second Series, Sheffield: Sheffield Academic Press, pp. 48–66.

VanderKam, J. C. (ed.) (1992) *'No One Spoke Ill of Her': Essays on Judith*, Atlanta, GA: Scholars Press.

Vermes, G. (1973) *Scripture and Tradition in Judaism*, Leiden: Brill.

Watson, F. (2000) *Agape, Eros, Gender: Towards a Pauline Sexual Ethic*, Cambridge: Cambridge University Press.

Weedon, C. (1999) *Feminism, Theory and the Politics of Difference*, Oxford: Blackwell.

Wegner, J. Romney (1988) *Chattel or Person? The Status of Women in the Mishnah*, Oxford: Oxford University Press.

Weir, A. (1996) *Sacrificial Logics: Feminist Theory and the Critique of Identity*, London: Routledge.

White, S. A. (1992) 'In the Steps of Jael and Deborah: Judith as Heroine', in J. Y VanderKam (ed.) *'No One Spoke Ill of Her': Essays on Judith*, Atlanta, GA: Scholars Press, pp. 5–16.

Whyte, A. (1905) *Bible Characters: Gideon to Absalom*, Edinburgh and London: Oliphant, Anderson & Ferrier.

Williams, D. S. (1993) *Sisters in the Wilderness: The Challenge of Womanist God-Talk*, Maryknoll, NY: Orbis Books.

Wire, A. (1991) 'Gender Roles in a Scribal Community', in D. L. Balch (ed.) *Social History of the Matthean Community: Cross Disciplinary Approaches*, Minneapolis, MN: Fortress Press, pp. 87–121.

Wolde, E. van (1997) 'Intertextuality: Ruth in Dialogue with Tamar' in A. Brenner and C. Fontaine (eds) *A Feminist Companion to Reading the Bible: Approaches, Methods and Strategies*, Sheffield: Sheffield Academic Press.

Wyke, M. (ed.) (1998) *Gender and the Body in the Ancient Mediterranean*, Oxford: Blackwell.

York, A. (1996) 'The Maturation Theme in the Adam and Eve Story' in J. E. Coleson and V. H. Matthews (eds) *'Go to the Land I Will Show You': Studies in Honor of Dwight W. Young*, Winona Lake, IN: Eisenbrauns.

SUBJECT AND
AUTHOR INDEX

172

INDEX OF TEXTS